Sprouting Again

a novel

Kayode Taiwo Olla

SYNCTERFACE

SYNCTERFACE MEDIA
London, UK
www.syncterfacemedia.com

Sprouting Again

ISBN: 978-0-9569741-1-2
Copyright © November 2011 by Kayode Taiwo Olla
All Rights Reserved

Published in the United Kingdom by

SYNCTERFACE™

Syncterface Media
London

www.syncterfacemedia.com
info@syncterfacemedia.com

Cover Design by Syncterface Media

Cover Picture by Klicks Digital, Nigeria
Author Photograph by Megatrends, Nigeria

To the memory of my father,

Oyebanji Olla

If I could stay that final breath at that old age,

I still would have, till a date that will never come!

'For there is hope for a tree, if it is cut down,

that it will sprout again,

and that its shoot will not cease.

Though its root grows old in the earth,

and its stump dies in the ground,

yet at the scent of water it will bud

and put forth branches like a young plant'

(Job XIV. 7 - 9, NRSV)

Acknowledgement

This book wouldn't have been a dream come true, without the help of some people. I wish to thank my darling mum, Adebomi – thanks a lot for your priceless support. You're just too irreplaceable! Also, my lovely brothers and sisters – Big sis Motunrayo, my twin Kehinde, and Damilola and Olaolu the younger twins – thanks for your valuable suggestions and all your encouragements. You're really wonderful! My brother-in-law and my big sister, Akin and Bukola Akinyemi – thank you for your assistance with the first publishing. Let me put it this way – thanks for being an uncle and a big sis that you are! Together with everyone at Syncterface Media, London – thank you all. You guys are great, I can say that!

Everyone should have a spiritual father and instructor like Pastor Peter Ilesanmi – thanks for helping me discover and build up my gift of writing. I must also thank Pastor Joel Oke and Pastor Shola Ajagbe, Principal and Vice-Principal, respectively, of The Redeemed Christian School of Missions, Ede, Osun State, Nigeria – thanks for welcoming me to write in the sequestered environment of your campus. The scenic beauty was really an inspiration. Lastly, Deacon E. A. Oke and Dr. K. Ayoola – thank you for taking time out to review the manuscript; I really appreciate it.

Thank you all.

Endorsements

You really have good prospects.

~ Dr. Kehinde Ayoola ~
Doctor of English,
Obafemi Awolowo University, Ile-Ife,
and author of *Healing Power of Love*

Sprouting Again – a story of circumstance, 'fate', and faith….
The use of language is really artistic and impressive for a first
work. Kayode Olla has surely come to stay!

~ Hannah Ojo ~
Winner of *The Nations*–Coca-Cola 2009 Reporter of the Year,
Best Campus-Life Opinion Writer Award

'*Sprouting Again* is a delightful mixture of tale and realism.
It is a reflection of God's love to us and of hope. I encourage
everyone to read this novel as it rebuilds hope and reassures us
that it's not over yet – there's hope!'

~ Mallam Adisa Stephen ~
Mobilisation Director,
Mission Volunteers International
Nigeria, Cameroon, Chad, Benin, Niger

Contents

Part One

1

Nothing Again

'But why, God? Why?' Romoke sighed, the expression on her face oozing a feeling of despondency.

She moved her *fitila*[1] closer and stared at the piece of paper in her hands which contained a piece of typed information. Then she read the content over and over again as a tear trickled down her face.

'Why this time? Why now? Why, God?' she asked rhetorically.

She turned and gazed at the little and tender baby sleeping serenely beside her on a blanket spread on the straw mat.

'But why can't my father understand?' she wondered in whispers. 'Saturday is the day and we're already in Wednesday. Saturday will soon come – a day that should at least bring consolation to me in my plight. Ah! My sun is setting at daytime! God, why now? Why this time?'

A cock crowed at the backyard. Then another from afar;

---

1 An oil lamp

then yet another from the frontage of the old mud house where Romoke was, pondering.

It was the early cockcrow of a Wednesday in late 1976 at a Yoruba village of south-western Nigeria called Ibupęsǫ. Doors of the mud houses of the village were still shut – obviously, the village was still asleep, but for a few women walking down the path leading to the village stream, with empty earthen pots carried under their arms. Some mothers had babies strapped to their backs, as the women walked in twos and threes to fetch water from the quiet, warm stream. Most of them only tied wrappers of *Ankara* cloth around their bodies, leaving their shoulders bare. Some were bare-footed while others had pairs of flip-flops on. They appeared to be sharing the experiences of the day before as they walked along.

But then again, that teenage girl Romoke woke up that day only in gloom. She seemed to be in a dilemma. But what could be so burdensome on her mind that it couldn't be shared with anyone but only pondered on in a soliloquy? And she sat alone in her room, with the sleeping baby, ruminating dejectedly.

But how did I get myself into this mess in the first place? I'm indeed the greatest fool on earth! But why at this time when my hopes are coming true?

'Ah!' she sighed.

Romoke was evidently faced with a dilemma. She had just got an admission into the University of Ijesha, Ijesha town; on the other hand, she just had a baby. The dilemma of either choosing to stay at home to nurse her baby and forgo her admission into the university or opting for the university at the expense of nursing her baby, was enough a worry for her. However, this was not the main cause of her sombreness. Moreover, she had her baby out of wedlock, and she was but eighteen. This, again, was less of a worry to her compared to the actual cause of her lugubrious mood.

As she sat still on the mat, the ultimatum of her strict father, a disciplinarian, echoed in her mind's ear:

Romoke, take it from me – if by Saturday, when the baby should be named, you hadn't made the father of the baby known to us and brought him to us, I swear, I will send you, together with your child, packing out of this house; and, look, I'll never send you to your university with my money – over my dead body – till you produce the baby's father! You mark me! I can't be a grandfather to a child without a father!

She let out a sigh.

'What do I do now? I'm in a fix. I'm in a tight corner. Hm, how do I know who the father is, for pity's sake? If I know who is actually, wouldn't I have told him? Mm, where do I go from here? How do I tackle this problem now?'

Odo-Akan, a town about a kilometre away from Ibupẹsọ had the only secondary school in that area. Romoke had led a promiscuous life in her final class in Odo-Akan Grammar School. She had messed herself up with many boys; and now she was reaping alone the seeds she had sown. Actually, she had had sex with nine boys, at about the same time, which resulted in a bastard child, as some might call it. At times, she might have sex with a boy on four different occasions. So then, it was difficult to know who the child's actual father was.

Moreover, in Ibupẹsọ village in those years, civilization was yet to be born and technology was still a stranger. So then, the determination of paternity by the alleged father's genetic content, the DNA (*Deoxyribonucleic acid*), was not yet known let alone being thought of as a way out.

'How did I get myself into this mess?' Romoke asked herself again. 'I wasn't like this before. At least I loved the Lord and devoted my life to Him. I gave my life to Him completely when I was thirteen, through Auntie Kikelomo, my uncle's wife. And Auntie Kike led me in the ways of God. But what actually went wrong? When did I start to derail before going this far? The dog that would eventually get lost, the elders say, will not hear the hunter's whistle – ah!'

She paused a bit after giving a sigh of worry. She looked

at her baby sleeping. She looked at him awhile, and then at the piece of paper in her hand which contained her admission letter into the university. She shook her head in regret and then continued in her mind-revealing monologue.

'God, You made me a girl with a bright promising future; if not for Felicia Ayelangbe who has thus ruined it – oh, she's ruined my life! I curse the day I met you, Felicia! How I wish I had never met you! Had I known you were a venomous snake, I wouldn't have made friends with you in the first place!'

She paused a bit and placed her palm under her chin, resting her chin on it.

'Mm, Felicia Ayelangbe,' she mused. 'She came to retake her Senior School Certificate Exam in my school, in Odo-Akan Grammar School – it was an exam of which I too was a candidate. She was a fashion-conscious girl, with very fashionable jewellery and expensive cosmetics in her wardrobe. But she was a lure – enticing bait! Had I known, I would have stood aloof to that girl, an enticing poison in person! She really influenced me with her immoral life. She gradually introduced me to having boyfriends, and then into having sex till I couldn't do without sex! And those boys I had affairs with then, all of them are now beyond reach. Many of them, after our final exam, had gone to big towns and cities – some of them should be in higher institutions by now, I suppose; but I once heard that a few have quit schooling. Ah! I'm nothing but a big fool – the biggest fool! They used me, dumped me and they go on with their lives! Ah!'

She paused for a long while, and suddenly she had an idea dropped into her spirit. She pondered on it awhile.

'No! How can I!?' she objected at once.

But… but, that may be the only way out.

She paused to ponder.

Aloud she said at once, 'No, that would be sheer wickedness, and God would be displeased and angry with me!'

She paused a bit.

But isn't God already angry with me?

'Oh yes – and to add this less serious sin to my many sins of having sex with many boys, will only make Him only slightly grieved more than He'd already been! After all, there's nothing I can do to help it; I'm only a human.'

She paused a bit.

A cock crowed outside. She stood up and went to the window – a very small wooden type, which could be shut or flung open. She opened it, held it ajar and looked outside. She hurriedly shut it back.

'Ha! I must be quick; the day's breaking! My father and mother will soon wake up.'

She went to her sleeping baby and, leaning forward, stretched her hand, which was visibly shaking, to carry him. But she couldn't for the pricking of her conscience. Tears gathered in her eyes.

Hmm, but what else can I do? I've got no option. My father is ready to disown me. My education, my admission   they are at stake. My dreams are beginning to drown before my very eyes! I've got… I've got no option.

'God, You should try to understand!' she said aloud.

Romoke knelt gently beside the baby and carried him. The baby woke and cried. She patted him gently and a tear rolled down her own cheek.

'I hope You'll forgive me, God. I hope You'll understand,' she wished as she wiped the tear with the back of her hand.

She gently opened the door and walked quietly through the gloomy corridor of the old mud house. She stopped at the door of her parents' bedroom and peeped through the keyhole. She saw them still asleep on the mat, and then she went out gently through the backyard door.

It was fifteen minutes to five at dawn that Wednesday and

Romoke trekked the distant path to a neighbouring village called Akatape, her heart audibly pounding as she walked along.

As she was approaching Akatape village, her conscience pricked her more. She sobbed quietly with a feeling of gloom but walked on resolutely.

She got to the village at about twenty past five that morning. It was still quiet. Few villagers had already woken up, but she ensured that she wasn't seen or monitored by anyone.

On arriving at Akatape village, she trod a narrow pathway amidst thick bush, with a view to carrying out her plans in secrecy. Fear gripped her heart more and more as she trod the dark, lonely path. She was hearing some weird cry of birds – birds believed in Africa to be easily possessed by witches' spirits. She became very terrified. She dreaded being confronted by an aje^2 or by $iwin^3$ or by the awo^4 who normally make their rituals in the dead night. She also thought of being attacked by wild animals. However, she summoned courage and entered into a deserted bushy farmland, and then she stopped by a big tree there.

Looking up into the sombre skies, she asked with a despairing tone, 'Where are You, God? Where?' All she could see was nothing but twinkling stars in the Galaxy that appeared like a million glistering diamonds and the moon, like a thousand times magnified pearl, gleaming softly.

She knelt down and gently placed the little baby, wrapped up securely in swaddling clothes, by the foot of the tree. The baby would cry but she sat near him and patted him till he slept off again.

Romoke looked for a long while into the baby's firmly shut melting eyes. She couldn't contain herself at the sight of those innocent sleeping eyes of the poor baby. Tears welled up in her eyes and she wiped them with the back of her hand.

---

2 Witch.
3 Spirits believed to live inside forests, clad in a palm frond skirt.
4 A traditional cult among the Yoruba, clad in white.

After a while, she got up gently and began to speak to the baby in whispers as though it heard and understood her.

Tears gathered in her eyes as she spoke.

'I know it's a bad thing I'm doing by dumping you here. I do not wish to do this. I don't wish to! But you know, you know – what else can I do? I wish I had the courage to hold on to you! If only I can keep you! But… but, I've got no option. I've… I've got no… I've got no option.'

She burst into tears.

At that same time, a sixty-two year old woman was at a stone's throw on the farmland. She wore a *buba*[5] and tied a wrapper around her body, from her chest downwards. She was fairly grey-haired and had a fairly wrinkled face. Her skin was sun tanned and rough. She had a chewing stick in her mouth which she was chewing as she gathered the sticks.

The old woman was picking sticks for firewood in this bush. She was gathering the sticks to cook for her youngest daughter who was just delivered of a baby.

As the old woman gathered the sticks in the early hours of that Wednesday, she seemed to hear someone talking in that bushy environment. She at first ignored it, thinking that it only seemed so. But when she heard the person beginning to cry, she was somewhat frightened.

There must be something terrifying around here.

'Ha, can it be *iwin* that live inside trees?' she said. 'Or maybe it is *ọrọ ọgẹdẹ*[6]. Or could it be that the *emere*[7] are having their meeting inside a tree over there? – but it is dawn now; it's not midnight, their usual time of meetings. I'll go and see whatever this thing is.'

She walked quietly towards the area where she could hear the sobs coming from. She forgot her pair of flip-flops behind.

---

5 A simple top
6 Spirits believed to talk from inside banana plants
7 A particular sect of witches in Yoruba land.

She didn't even sense that she was bare-footed, as it was habitual for old rustics to walk without shoes.

When she was at close range to Romoke, she stopped. She was only separated from her by thickets. She watched Romoke intently through the small spaces in between the closely packed bushes. She could see a tall teenage girl. The girl was dark in complexion and was dressed in a sky-blue nightdress, and she wore her hair in plaits. She had a slender, attractive figure and a supple body with perfect curves.

The old woman watched Romoke quietly, wondering who she was and what her problem could be that she stood there that dawn, weeping. She saw her quite well but she didn't look down to see the baby at the foot of the tree, as the thicket blocked her view of it. Romoke, though, was oblivious of the old woman secretly watching her.

'I did not intend to do this,' continued Romoke in a barely audible voice, 'but I'm left with no option – no other way out of my plight.'

She paused to wipe a tear from her eyes.

'If only', she continued, 'my father was not a strict man, or rather, if only he hadn't given the ultimatum – or, better still, if only you my baby hadn't come at such a time like this – no, if only I had not involved myself in pre-marital sex –' She burst into tears. 'I', she concluded amidst tears, 'would not be in such a predicament as this, that I now have no option than to do this evil thing!'

At that juncture, the old woman concluded that Romoke was likely to be a girl who would need encouraging words; for she had earlier thought her insane. She then decided to approach her but she remembered that she had forgotten her pair of flip-flops where she was gathering firewood. So, she decided to go first to take them as well as secure the firewood, tying them together in a bundle so that whoever got there would know that it belonged to someone.

She quickly but quietly went to her firewood.

At this time, Romoke was already saying her parting words to her baby as she bade it farewell forever.

'… And now that I will abandon you, I doubt if your innocent soul will ever forgive me. I doubt if God too will ever pardon me. But I plead with your innocent soul – hm – please, please bear with me. God watch over you while I can no more watch! Bye-bye!'

And as she waved slowly and walked away from there, rather slowly, looking back again and again, tears welled up in her eyes and a yearning from the bowels of her heart; but no, she wouldn't go back, as she was in the extremity of desperation as she saw her academic dreams and prospects beginning to crumble in her very eyes! But what an inhuman thing to resort to!

After a couple of minutes, the old woman, having finished bundling up her firewood, taken her pair of flip-flops and put them on, appeared where Romoke had been but discovered that the sad girl had disappeared!

'Goodness! I stayed too long behind!' she exclaimed.

As she wanted to go after the girl, she was deeply shocked at the sight of the poor baby abandoned under the big tree in that secluded bushy area in the early hours of that Wednesday morning.

'Ah! *Ikunḷẹ abiamọ o!*[8] ' she exclaimed, with her two hands on her head. 'Ha, so that is what this girl was up to! What a cruel act! Ah, I must go after her right away!'

She took off her pair of flip-flops so that they wouldn't disturb her as she was prepared to run or move a fast as possible, and not even minding her age that she wasn't a youth and that those feeble legs of hers were ageing and no more as agile as they were some thirty-four years earlier when she was Romoke's age! She made a dash for the footpath leading out of the farmland. No sooner had she taken three strides than she

8 A Yoruba exclamation used when you see a catastrophe.

stubbed her big toe against one of the tree's big roots that was just by the baby; and it started to bleed quite a lot.

'Yeh, my leg!' she exclaimed out of pain.

The baby, disturbed, started to cry. She rushed for a banana branch from a banana plant close by and squeezed its liquid from the leaf stalk on the bleeding wound. This, in a typical village like this, is known to be medicinal and efficacious in healing fresh bleeding cuts.

Not long after the old woman applied the liquid from the banana leaf stalk on the bleeding wound, the bleeding stopped as the blood clotted; however, it had stained the swaddling clothes with which the baby was wrapped, very much.

But why this injury? Perhaps this is cautioning me not to pick up the poor baby – but could it be? Oh the girl might actually come back to pick it, I guess.

At that time, the cry of the baby was intensifying. The old woman, with a gleam of compassion and affection in her eyes, looked at the baby, whose swaddling clothes had been stained all over with blood – she looked at the baby for quite a while. Then she hurried to her firewood and picked up a little cloth she had rolled together into a fold.

'Yes, this *oṣuka*⁹ should equally serve the purpose. I think I'll use it.'

She dusted the *oṣuka* and rushed back to the baby.

'Sorry, my dear; I'm back. I've got another cloth to wrap your tender body with,' she said.

She carried the baby gently, removed its blood-stained swaddling clothes and threw it to the ground. Then she wrapped the baby with her old cloth – her *oṣuka*.

She carried him warmly against her bosom and patted him; and he ceased to cry. The baby then put its breast-milk-thirsty

---

9 Any piece of cloth that is rolled together and placed on the head when carrying a load on the head.

lips at the old woman's breast. Pity and sympathy welled up from the bowel of her heart.

'Oh, poor little thing!' she said.

She took away the baby's lips from her breast. Then she felt a deep sense of responsibility for the poor child. She felt an impression at this gesture of the breast-milk-thirsty 'motherless' child, that God was bidding her to adopt him.

'It's all right; I'll take him home,' mused the old woman. 'Asake will nurse him for me while she nurses her own baby.'

The old woman was in Akatape village to stay with and help her youngest daughter Asake, who had just given birth. She therefore was going to persuade her to nurse this baby for her together with her own.

So, from that time, Romoke's baby became the old woman's adopted child.

* * *

The day had broken; the villagers of Ibupẹsọ, Romoke's village, had then awoken. The sun was rising and the melodious bird song emanating from the village trees was beginning to pervade the village air. The golden sun rays had started to pierce the early morning mist, revealing a picturesque village of clusters of rusty corrugated-iron-roofed mud houses. The golden sun rays also adorned the jungle greenery and gilded the warm village stream.

Farmers were heading to their farmlands, dressed in shabby working clothes. Each held a cutlass in his hand and hanged a hoe on his shoulder. Some had dogs going ahead of them and many had little boys also going in front of them, carrying empty straw baskets, turned upside down on their heads. Women were heading towards the streams, carrying empty earthen pots, to fetch water with them. Most of them were dressed in buba and wrapper, but tied the wrapper from the chest downwards. Most of them walked bare-footed, while others wore flip-flops.

In a small compound of clusters of mud houses, stood an old mud house facing the road. The frontage of the old mud house was crowded with worried and confused neighbours. The house was that of Romoke's family. Her father, Delakin Bayetiri, was a tall, dark and well built man of about fifty, who had tribal marks on his cheeks. He dressed only in a *kembe*[10] and without a *buba*, and he was furiously pacing the frontage of the house. Romoke's mother, Segilola, was a light-complexioned woman of about forty, small-statured also with tribal marks on her cheeks. She had a wrapper tied around her body, revealing tattoos on her bare shoulders and arms. And she was in utter perplexity concerning her daughter and the baby's whereabouts. They kept on enquiring from the neighbours if anyone had seen Romoke that day and many concerned neighbours had gone searching for her in the length and breadth of Ibupęsǫ village; but no one knew where she was, for nobody had set eyes on her that day.

'But where could she have gone for goodness' sake?' wondered the worried mother, Segilola.

'Let her just come home quickly, and I'll beat sense into her!' shouted the angry father. 'Or who does she think she can cause needless worry, uh?' His voice dropped. 'I have been to Dekunle my brother; I thought she would be in his house for certain, but she wasn't there – you can't find her footprints there!'

'Ah! So, she's not even in your younger brother's place?' asked Segilola.

'No, not at all!'

'But where else can we look for her?'

'I don't know; I just don't know!'

'What makes me more disturbed is the little baby she carried along to where no one knows at this early time of the

---

10 A short pair of trousers with wide legs.

day!' said the mother worriedly.

'And she never at anytime told anyone where she was going?' queried one of the neighbours standing there.

'No, she just vanished like smoke in the air!' replied Delakin the father, his voice still depicting fury.

'Not even you, *Mama Rọmọke[11]* ?' asked another neighbour.

'No, not anyone!' she replied.

Kikelomo, Romoke's uncle's wife, was then approaching the worried crowd that was gathered in the frontage of Romoke's house. She was a tall, dark and slender woman of thirty-one, dressed in a *buba* and tied a wrapper around her body. She was holding her head tie in her hand, which she had loosened from her head to allow for fresh air on her head. She was breathing at a rather fast pace as she approached the anxious crowd. She had gone searching for Romoke in Odo-Akan Grammar School – the school where Romoke finished from, in Odo-Akan town; but she couldn't find her there.

When she told the neighbours gathered at the frontage of Romoke's house, that Romoke was not in Odo-Akan Grammar School, where they again thought she could be, they became more disturbed.

'But why can't we search for her in Akatape?' suggested Kikelomo. 'Who knows whether that's where she went!'

Delakin, still in a fury, rebuffed the suggestion. 'What will she do there? Do we have anybody in Akatape?'

'Don't say that, *Baale mi,[12]*' said Segilola; 'a person searches for a lost thing anyhow – let's try.'

'I think I should go right away,' said Kikelomo.

'No, you'll be too tired for such a long trek as that to Akatape, said Segilola – 'stay behind; some other person will go.'

---

11 Romoke's Mum.
12 My lord

'No, mama, I think there's still strength in me to take me to Akatape and back,' explained Kikelomo – 'let me quickly go.'

'All right – go well; may *Eleduwa*[13] grant you success,' said Segilola.

Kikelomo began heading towards Akatape village. As she went along, she mused, 'I pray I will find her. I pray God will guide her steps back home.'

At that time, Romoke was nearing Ibupẹsọ. But at each step farther from Akatape, and at each step nearer to Ibupẹsọ, her conscience smote her, and the fear of getting home to meet a father whose fiery fury could consume her, gripped her more.

It seemed the gravity of that wicked act of hers of throwing away her innocent baby was dawning on her like never before. Her conscience pricked her sorely and her heart yearned very much for her poor, innocent child.

At this point, Kikelomo, who was already exiting Ibupẹsọ village, sighted Romoke, who was at a long distance away. She noticed that she was not with her baby and that she was downcast.

Something must be wrong.

But during all this, Romoke had not noticed her aunt, for she (Romoke) was walking despondently with a downcast gaze.

As Romoke's conscience smote her more and more, producing in her heart an unbearable surge of guilt, she suddenly made a turn and headed for Akatape again to carry her baby.

Kikelomo noticed her sudden turn and thought she had seen her; but because she still walked slowly rather than take to her heels, she concluded that she had not noticed her. So Kikelomo walked fairly faster to catch up with Romoke.

While she was at a stone's throw from her, Kikelomo called, 'Romoke dear!'

---

13 The Almighty

Romoke looked back to see who called. On seeing her uncle's wife, she wanted to run, but Kikelomo gave a confidence assuring smile; and so she stopped.

'Romoke, what's wrong? You should look happy everytime,' she said, deliberately avoiding asking her about the baby, to gain her confidence. 'Is something the matter, my girl?'

'No, Auntie Kike; nothing.'

'Nothing? Are you sure?'

'Yes… I… I think so.'

'You think so? No, you don't feel shy, my dear. Tell me, is something wrong?'

'Erm – Auntie Kike, you can't help in this; you would do well to leave me to my plight.'

'Don't say that. Look, a trouble shared is a trouble halved. He who keeps silent, their plight will also stay comfortably with them, the elders say.'

'No, Auntie; not for this kind – sharing will rather worsen the whole situation.'

'I know what you mean, Romoke dear. But look, keeping mute may not help; it may not improve the situation. As a matter of fact, once you share your problems, though there may be seemingly bigger ones that may appear to loom large, yet you will eventually overcome them and smile when you discover they are only paper tigers! And can paper tigers bite?'

Kikelomo placed her hand on Romoke's shoulder and looked into her eyes. 'An issue cannot be so hard that you need to cut it with a knife – you simply have to share it. More so, the banana plant is not up to what you confront with a machete!'

Kikelomo had developed a close rapport with Romoke, especially during this time of her loneliness and despondency since her father had begun to be harsh to her concerning the paternity of her child.

Romoke looked into Kikelomo's eyes. She wondered why

her aunt did not ask her about her baby.

She should be a good confidant. I think I can confide in her.

She breathed a deep sigh. 'Can I tell you something shocking, Auntie?' she asked.

'Shocking? Oh, why not?

Romoke started to narrate the story to her aunt, stammeringly. When she got to the most crucial but most absurd and anger-provoking part of her story, she hesitated for fear.

'Go on, Romoke,' said Kikelomo encouragingly.

'So I... I went to Akatape and... and abandoned the... the baby at a bush there.'

'Huh! Did what!?'

Kikelomo stared blankly at her in a stunned silence and shivered as though the air around her had suddenly gone cold.

Kikelomo used to be barren for a period of four years before she had had her only child, a boy, who did not live to see his naming day; and since then, she 'had never had a protuberant stomach': thus, her inability to contain the shock.

She sank slowly on the ground as she just managed to say, 'My God! My God!' in a low, trembling voice. Romoke burst into tears as she again realised the weight and gravity of her wrong, causing her to feel guiltier.

After a while of Kikelomo's stunned silence, she made an effort to get her emotions normalised, and she stood up and patted Romoke on the shoulder, encouraging her.

'There's still hope, my girl; don't cry.'

'Hope? Auntie, my hope is lost!'

'Course not, you have hope. Where do you say you threw the baby?'

'In Akatape – at an abandoned farmland,' Romoke replied, stretching her finger towards Akatape.

'All right,' said Kikelomo; 'let's go right away. Lead me

there. You just keep begging God as we go.'

They both headed towards Akatape village at a fast pace – sometimes walking, sometimes running.

And at last, they arrived at the deserted farmland in Akatape, but lo and behold, the baby was no longer there! They were stunned!

'Ah! My God! But that's where I left the baby! Ah! I'm finished!'

Kikelomo went near the tree and saw the swaddling clothes on the ground. 'The swaddling clothes are still there,' she said – 'someone might have picked up the baby.' But as she went to pick up the swaddling clothes, she noticed something very shocking – blood stains on the swaddling clothes! 'AH!!! The baby is dead!'

'What, Auntie!?'

'Look,' said Kikelomo, stretching the blood-stained swaddling clothes to her.

'Ah! A wild animal has killed my baby!' cried Romoke.

Kikelomo grew furious with Romoke and was filled with burning anger towards her – such that a reasonable woman would have towards such an inhumane, callous girl, or rather, young mother.

She rebuked her with a harsh tone. 'Are you not the one who handed your baby over to the wild animals!?' Her visage itself bespoke this burning anger.

Romoke stared at her aunt speechless. She had never seen her so furious.

'You killed the baby yourself directly or indirectly!' she continued. 'I can't keep the truth from you, my dear. I must tell you the bitter truth if I truly love you! You have done a very bad thing, Romoke; in fact, one of the most terrible things to do, of which you must start to beg God for mercy, or else!'

Kikelomo displayed a high degree of feminine tenderness.

Her lips never wanted sweet encouraging words, though she herself was not without problems, as she did bear the sorrow of childlessness. She had not been a positive-thinking, optimistic, undeterred woman from the outset but her sorrows of being childless had made that of her.

'What will I do now? My father will tear me into pieces when I get home!' sobbed Romoke.

'My girl, you have to take the bull by the horns. We will go back home now and you'll have to tell your parents so that –'

'Tell my parents!?'

'Of course,you have to, dear – look, the earlier they know, the better for you. And in fact, you cannot just hide it from them!'

'Ah! I am done for!'

'No, don't make a negative confession about yourself. Look, you have to let your parents know. I promise that I will support you – by that, I mean I'll stand by you. I'll beg for you – you don't worry; all is going to be well.'

Steadily they walked home, taking the swaddling clothes along, as Kikelomo rolled them together and wrapped her head tie around it.

When they arrived at Romoke's house, everyone began to bombard her with questions and rebukes; but Kikelomo asked Romoke's father to allow Romoke to narrate everything to him and her mother in private, and also that she herself be allowed in with them.

When with her parents and in the company of her aunt, Romoke narrated everything stammering, as her aunt encouraged her to go on each time she stopped for fear.

At the end of her narration, when the parents knew that Romoke had thrown away her baby and, on seeing the blood-stained swaddling clothes, concluded that the baby had been devoured by some wild beast, her father's fury blazed like a dry bush set on fire in the harmattan season; while her mother collapsed like an iroko tree struck by a thunderbolt, but she was soon revived.

Now, Dekunle, Romoke's uncle and Kikelomo's husband,entered seeing his younger brother, Romoke's father, shouted, 'Dekunle, you see who I call my daughter? You see – my daughter? Thrown baby away – wild animal killed it – silly story! You see! If you don't take this girl out of my sight now, I will do what all of you will be surprised at. I will wound her with my machete – you all think I can't do it!'

Kikelomo tried hustling Romoke out.

'Leave her,' Dekunle said to her softly. He turned to his older brother.'*Ẹgbọn*[14] , I don't understand what you are saying; but whatever be the case, you can discipline your daughter, but the issue of wounding your own daughter with a machete if she doesn't leave your sight ah-ah –come on, forget that!'

'My what? I have *no* daughter, *no* child henceforth!' shouted Delakin. 'I disown her, and I mean it!'

'Disown *your* daughter?' queried Dekunle, wondering.

'If you care, take her as your daughter,' replied Delakin – 'She is no longer the daughter of me, Adelakin son of Bayetiri. She may now be the daughter of Adekunle Bayetiri – but never mine!'

There was an awkward silence. Dekunle bowed his head, not knowing what to say.

'Take this girl out my sight, I say!' shouted Delakin, breaking the silence.

When no one made a move, he dashed into one small room and out he came with a sharp, glistering machete, brandishing it in the air.

'Does she want to dare me? Let her stay!' he roared. He put the blade briskly in his mouth and bit it: 'I swear by Ogun the god of iron, I will leave a lasting scar on her body with this!

---

14 Big brother.

Let her dare me!'

Everybody ran out, leaving Segilola, Romoke's mother, alone with Delakin. She stood up and went closer to her husband.

'*Olowo ori mi*[15] ,' she said, 'I think we should handle this situation with love, rather than with outburst of anger which may not help the matter but rather worsen it.'

'Leave me, woman!' shouted Delakin.

'But...but... I plead with you, *Baalemi*,' she continued as she went on her knees, 'for my sake, pardon her please. *Temi ni ki ẹ wo!*[16] ' she entreated.

'Leave me, woman!' Delakin shouted again, with more vehemence.

Segilola held her husband's *kẹmbẹ* and began to beg for her daughter most earnestly. '*Ọkọ mi, Baale mi, Olowo ori mi!* [17] It is your wife and the mother of your only daughter and child that pleads. For my sake, your dear wife, please pardon your daughter. Think of my nine months of carrying her in my womb. Think of my maternal blood at her birth, and of the labour pains. Think of my one and a half years of breast feeding her. Think of my three years of strapping her to my back. Adelakin my husband, *dakun jọ 'ọ —*[18] '

Delakin Bayetiri, whose heart was already melting at the sweet words of his good wife and that carefully presented rendition of a plea by that compassionate mother, dropped his machete and raised her up. He held her by her shoulders, looked a while into her eyes with affection and said: 'Segilola my dear wife, I am very proud to have you as my wife. Honestly, I feel very unworthy that I, being an angry, impatient and harsh man, should have you, a soft-hearted, tender and compassionate "goddess", as wife! You're to me like Ọṣun the goddess of

15 The one who paid my bride price.
16 Do it for my sake.
17 My husband, My Lord, The one who paid my bride price.
18 Please and please.

children – like she was to her hot-tempered husband, Ṣango the god of thunder and lightning! I'm very proud of you!' And he embraced her.

'Will my lord then take Romoke back as his daughter?' enquired Segilola.

'Erm, I'll… I'll think it over,' he replied.

* * *

At that time, Romoke was in her uncle's house, crying.

'I'm left with no more hope – not one ray of hope left!' she said to Kikelomo, who was sitting by her, consoling her.

'Don't say that, Romoke. God is the Hope of the hopeless,' Kikelomo consoled.

'God! Of course, I know that. But do I have God? I mean, do I have Him anymore? I have sinned. I have long wandered from His path you once laid my feet on, Auntie. I don't have Him anymore and I don't have hope.'

'Don't say that; don't confess negative things,' said Kikelomo.

'Auntie, you don't understand. I have lost everything already; I'm left with nothing else. I have lost my baby and lost my opportunity for admission into university; my father has disowned me – I have even lost the inner witness I used to have before the whole thing started, that I'm a child of God. Now, there's nothing again! NOTHING AGAIN!!'

'You've lost everything, right?' queried Kikelomo. 'But a saying rightly expresses God's verdict on your plight, like this: "Where there is life, there is hope" – my dear, have you lost life too?'

Romoke looked into the eyes of her sage aunt, as she also looked into hers. She shook her head slowly, left and right.

'No, Auntie, I have life.'

'And so, my girl, there is hope!'

2

Same Words Again

'I am set, *Ma'a mi*[19]. I'm ready to go.'

Romoke's visage was alight. She was looking radiant with happiness. Her beauty which had been somewhat shrouded, as it were, around that same period three years earlier, by a gloomy mood was, this time around, unveiled by elation.

Three years had passed since Romoke lost her child– or rather, thrown him away; and the year was then gradually approaching its end: it was the last quarter of the year 1979.

Romoke who was standing inside the sitting room of her father's house, close to the doorway that opened to the frontage, and amidst few pieces of luggage of varying sizes, was beautifully dressed in a pink Western ready-made dress. She had a pair of black slingbacks on, and wore her hair in cornrows. And she wore a pair of golden studs in her ears.

---

19 Mum

'Wait, I'm coming – just a minute,' answered her mother who was coming out of the inner room into the sitting room, tying and untying her wrapper.

As she entered the sitting room, she stopped, and then gestured for Romoke to come near her for an embrace. She went near her mother and they embraced each other for a while.

After the warm mother-daughter embrace, Segilola said, 'Just one more thing my daughter – one last thing to say.'

She moved aside and went to the wooden window – this was a larger one than that of the bedroom – or mat-room, so to speak! The window was already open. She looked out, leaving Romoke standing in the centre of the sitting room, watching what her mother was about to do.

What we would have seen outside was the scorching African sun that afternoon, but no, she wasn't looking to the sky. We would have also seen the trees which were beginning to shed their dry leaves on the rain-thirsty soil. The dry season of 1979 was steadily approaching as the year was nearing its end.

But then again, the elderly woman was not concerned about the dryness that we would have noticed. She had actually gone to the window to look at something significant. We would of course have also seen a grave beside the house – this was exactly what she had gone to behold.

'You left us too soon,' she mused, wiping a tear from her eyes as she looked awhile at the grave. Then she went back to Romoke.

Romoke had known what brought those tears to her mother's eyes. Segilola placed her hand on her shoulder. She was looking very grave, as she was about to say some words so significant, so relevant.

'Remember the daughter of whom you are,' she said to her solemnly.

The words seemed to echo many times in Romoke's ears. They seemed to carry a deeper meaning to her than anyone would understand them to mean. They actually produced in her mind that moment a clear recollection of her father's parting moments to the silent land.

* * *

The stars were twinkling in the Galaxy and the moon glimmered softly. The croaking of frogs filled the cool village air. The year was 1978.

Delakin's family were deeply apprehensive as he, a once strong and robust man, lay a weakling on the straw mat in his room as a result of a terminal illness that made him quite emaciated. He lay in his room, putting on a ṣọọrọ[20] – he did not wear a buba[21], revealing his gaunt chest and arms.

Delakin was in a light sleep on the mat. Beside his mat on the ground was a calabash in which there was a concoction of herbs. At a corner in that room was a frame of curved twisted palm fronds and within which was a broad machete stuck into the ground, suggesting their place of oblation to Ogun the god of iron. Beside Delakin, on the mat, was Romoke, seated and sobbing softly as she gazed at her weak father; for she feared that he should die. At the backyard of the house was Segilola, also weeping.

Baba Oyeku, a native doctor expert in making people elude death at critical moments (for that was why he was called Ọyẹku, which is the name for the charm believed to be able to make people elude death), had made sacrifices and appeal on his behalf to the powers, but all to no avail.

'The powers have kept mute,' he had told them; 'they will not tell me what they will do. I have pleaded with them, but they will do only what they are disposed to do!'

20 A simple pair of trousers.
21 A simple top.

Segilola had been disturbed at that.

What if the powers are disposed to take him away? Ah, agbẹdọ[22]! But... but who dares question their word?

As Romoke sobbed, Delakin woke from his light sleep and looked into Romoke's red eyes. 'Why are you crying, Romoke?' he asked.

'*Ba'a mi[23]*, I don't want you to die! I don't want you to die!'Romoke sobbed.

'Is that why you're crying?' Delakin asked. 'You don't have to cry – *o ya[24]* , cheer up; cheer up, my daughter.'

Delakin mustered strength and sat up, resting his back against the wall.

Actually, Delakin had come to appreciate his daughter, especially since he became ill some six months earlier. Delakin had earlier sent her away from home to live with his younger brother when she threw away her baby. But it was during his illness when Romoke had come over to take care of him that he took her back fully, realising how caring a daughter she could be.

'Come near, my daughter, sit beside me here,' he said, gesturing to her.

Romoke moved closer, sitting beside her father on the mat and resting her back against the wall too. Then they had a father-daughter talk.

'...I have been without fatherly understanding and care all this while; I have failed to show you fatherly love. I never realised then that if a parent spanks his child with the left hand, he also draws the child closer with the right hand. Romoke, I'm really sorry for how harsh I have been to you. I now see what a caring girl you have proven to be at a time like this, not even considering how I mistreated you. Forgive

---

22 Never!
23 My father
24 Come on.

me, please; I am so sorry.'

'*Ba'a mi*, there's no problem,' replied Romoke. 'I'm not annoyed with you. You are my father, after all.'

'Ah, thank you, my daughter! How I now wish to send you to the university, but I have spent everything I have on this illness of mine that refuses to go… Call your mother for me.'

'Okay, *Ba'a mi*' replied Romoke and then dashed out of the room into the backyard. While Segilola was in the backyard, she looked up into the starry sky and saw a star fall from the Galaxy. Alarmed by this portent, she laid her hands on her head. 'Ah! The powers will not preserve him!' she exclaimed.

And immediately after, Romoke entered. '*Ma'a mi*, my father is calling you,' she said to her.

'Uh, what…what happened? What happened to him?' queried Segilola, suspecting that her husband Delakin had passed on.

'Nothing,' replied Romoke.

They both went in, only to meet him lying down on the mat with his eyes shut and his body motionless.

'Ah! *O ti ṣẹlẹ*[25]!' exclaimed Segilola.

He opened his eyes and grinned. 'It's not yet happened', he said, 'but it is happening!' And gesturing with his hand, he said, 'Come near, my wife. Romoke – you too come near.'

They went to him and sat down.

'Segilola, take good care of Romoke,' he said to his wife. 'Send her to the university as much as it is within your power to do so. I can sense my ancestors beckoning me from the world beyond –'

'Ah! *Irọ o!* [26]' exclaimed Romoke, interrupting.

---

25 Is happened.
26 Never

'Don't worry,' he continued; 'don't feel dejected. I am actually going to come back. Our forefathers asserted that those who died unfulfilled do come back to live their life again – Segilola and Romoke, you do not worry; I will reincarnate. But then, I may not be given the opportunity to be born again into this home; and if Obatala the god of creation has willed it that I will come to the earth again through this family, I will certainly not have the opportunity of being your father again, Romoke; or your husband again, Segilola. Surely when I reincarnate, I will make the best and wisest use of my life – I will not repeat the mistakes and failures of this first life.'

'Ba'a mi,' interrupted Romoke, 'I am sorry, but I have to tell you this. Let us stop deceiving ourselves, and face reality. If anyone dies, I'm afraid, there is no coming back to live their life again!'

'Will you keep quiet, my friend!' shouted Delakin, rather angrily.

'*Awu, Baba Romoke!*[27]' reproved Segilola. 'Let her say what she has to say.'

'*Ki l'omode mo?*[28]' Delakin scoffed.

'Continue *jare*[29] ,' said Segilola, gesturing to Romoke.

'It's just that', continued Romoke, 'I don't want *Ba'a mi* to get to the world beyond only to be disappointed, as there's no repentance in the grave! Auntie Kike has always told me that after death then judgement comes. The truth is that a person has only one life, *Ba'a mi!*'

'Enough!' shouted Delakin. 'Where were you or Kikelomo when our great ancestors – I mean Oduduwa and his offspring, who were not age mates with the grandfather of your great grandfather – where were you when they discovered this fact? Anyway, let's close that chapter.'

---

27 Come on, Romoke's Dad
28 What does a child know?
29 Please

There was an awkward silence. Then after a while, Delakin began to cough and the cough grew more intense.

'Easy, *Ba'ami*,' said Romoke. 'Should I go for water?'

She did not wait for a response. She quickly dashed out of the room into the corridor and went to a corner where a large earthen pot, called *amu*, sat. She opened the lid on it and scooped the water in it, which was cool, with a calabash.

She dashed back into the room again, with the calabash of water in her hand, but her father had stopped coughing; and he was now sitting up.

'Here it is, *Ba'a mi,*' Romoke offered.

'Thank you my daughter. I am now alright,' replied Delakin. 'Sit down here beside me.'

She put down the calabash of water and sat down on the mat beside her father, facing him slightly.

Delakin placed his hand on Romoke's shoulder, looked straight into her eyes, and said 'Remember the daughter of whom you are' these were his last words. Shortly afterwards he began to gasp and soon bade this world farewell.

* * *

Back from her reminiscence, Romoke could not help but shed a tear. Segilola removed her hand from Romoke's shoulder, where she had placed it and she wiped a tear from her own eyes, for she was also shedding tears.

After a couple of minutes of thoughtful tears, her mother gave her solemn words of counsel as she was leaving for the University of Ijesha in Ijesha town, about eighteen kilometres away from Ibupẹsọ.

'Listen, my daughter, *ina eṣiṣi kii jo 'ni l'ẹẹmeji* [30]: beware of the recurrence of evil. I know you understand what I mean. In the campus over there – I have never been to one, but I

---

30 A Yoruba proverb synonymous to the English "Once bitten, twice shy"

know you will meet different types of people. Many bad boys will be there as well as bad girls. Some will come to entice you with sweet words – *alatiṣe nii mọ atiṣe ara rẹ[31]* . Do not allow anyone to ruin you again. All that glitters is not gold – not all the love young men show is true: beware! Above all, remember the daughter of whom you are!'

'Thank you, *Ma'a mi,*' Romoke said, kneeling down; 'I will keep these words in my heart.'

Romoke was very thankful for what her mother had done to send her to the university. Segilola was working at the local palm mill, where palm oil was locally made by boiling palm fruits and treading them in a cemented hollow with bare feet – a sort of rough, dirty job, as it were. It was from her income from this menial job, which was not in form of wages or salary but money realised from the sale of ten litres of palm oil given her for a day's job to sell, that she used to send her daughter to the higher institution as that was still insufficient. She had then sold virtually all her ceremonial attires which included her most cherished *aṣọ ofi* [32] that she wore for her traditional marriage to Romoke's father when she was twenty four years old, and which she had preserved since then and treasured. The *aṣọ ofi* she usually wore for the annual *Egungun*[33] festival was also included, among many others. She also gathered broad leaves, with Romoke help, and sold them to sellers of *mọin-mọin*[34], *akara*[35] and *ẹkọ*[36] .

'*Ma'a mi,*' continued Romoke, 'words cannot express my sincere thanks to you for labouring so much to send me to university. Thank you once again, ma.'

'It's a pleasure, my daughter. You can get up,' replied Segilola. 'Actually it is a mother's pleasure to labour for her

---

31 (Yoruba saying) It is the person with a problem that will know how to go about the problem.
32 A type of woven cotten material
33 Yoruba traditional masquerade
34 Cooked bean cakes
35 Fried bean cakes
36 Solid pap.

child when the child is young, that the child may labour for her when she is old.'

Romoke, having got up from her knees, carried her load outside. Some children in the neighbourhood helped her to carry most of them. They were excited that their 'big sister' was going to the university.

'Hey! Sister Romoke is going to the university!'

'Ah, we won't see her for a very long time!'

'Sister Romoke, when will you come back home to visit us? Or are there no holidays there like ours in the primary school?'

'Sister Romoke, please buy plenty of sweets and chewing gum for us whenever you are coming home.'

Romoke looked back and, with a broad smile, waved at her mother, who was standing at the doorway of their house and she also waved back again and again. Romoke and the children started trekking the one-kilometre-long sandy road to Odo-Akan town, where she would board a bus going to Ijesha town.

Romoke was looking back time and time again at her mother who was waving to her as she went farther and farther away. Her mother kept on waving and waving even when Romoke was no longer looking back. She kept on waving, tears gathering in her eyes, till Romoke was out of sight; and then she stopped and wiped her tears with her wrapper.

3

Crushed Again

'Now tell me, Francis: is anything the matter? You are not a dull student. Were you not on top of the class in your Year One? But what has gone wrong with you, uh? I have continuously asked you this same question for the last two sessions when I noticed your receding performance in your studies, but you always said everything was fine. Francis, does it now seem everything was actually fine, for you to drop out eventually? Uh, Francis?'

Francis Alantakun was a Year Three student of Mass Communication in the University of Ijesha in the previous session but had now dropped out. He was sitting in front of his head of department Dr. Emeka, with a downcast gaze as he talked with bafflement and concern.

The year was 1981 and the place was the office of the head of the department of Mass Communication, on the University of Ijesha campus, Ijesha town.

The office was well furnished and beautifully carpeted in red. A world map and a few paintings of some African artists adorned the wall. On the office desk was a black analogue telephone.

Francis Alantakun, a tall, dark and handsome twenty-six year old man was dressed casually in blue jeans, a light brown T-shirt and a pair of black sandals.

'Now tell me, Francis – what is actually wrong with you? Have you been sick – because I notice you have been looking dull and miserable for the last two sessions? Are you ill, Francis?'

Francis still kept mute, with his head bowed. He was trying to figure out what answer he should give to Dr. Emeka's question.

'Answer me, Francis! Am I not talking to you?' shouted Dr. Emeka.

'Ye… Yes, sir. I've been… I've been sick sir,' replied Francis in a stammer.

'And what type of sickness is this?' enquired Dr Emeka.

Francis was not able to answer.

'I hope you are taking good care of your health now,' he went on. 'But you should have, at least, told me that you have been unwell. Anyway, I hope you are taking all your medication as you should?'

'Yes… yes, sir. Thank you sir,' replied Francis.

What a clever man Francis Alantakun was! Had he really been sick? How smart to have given Dr. Emeka the impression that he had been sick all along! But, wait a moment, had he not been sick? Or was he not correct? At least, in his own clever way! Yes, he had actually been lovesick! Or rather, lust.

After Dr. Emeka's discussion with him, Francis thanked him for his concern, after which he left his office.

He came out of the department office block, looked back and gazed at the edifice awhile, and then moved on.

He walked slowly, dejected. He walked on one side of the

tarred street that led to the gigantic main gate, and looked at the office blocks and the tall trees that lined both sides of the street. He had to fight back the tears at the thought that he had dropped out. He looked at the hedge that were in vibrant greens and at the flowers that adorned the roadside as if perhaps he could find solace in their beauty. He gazed at the butterflies engaging in a display of their '*agbada*' of vibrant colours in front of the attractive hibiscus flowers which also displayed their red lips for a kiss.

And then he came to the main gate, on which was written boldly: THE UNIVERSITY OF IJESHA, IJESHA. On exiting the main gate, Francis saw someone – someone he believed was responsible for his plight. The person he saw was a light-complexioned, muscular and huge man of about thirty. He wore his hair in the afro style. He had a moustache and a pointed goatee. He had on a pair of dark glasses and wore a heavy gold chain around his neck. He was dressed in a fitted grey T-shirt on a pair of black bell-bottoms.

'Harry! Harry! Come; I want to see you!' Francis called out.

Harry saw Francis and stopped. He noticed Francis' dejected mood. He went to him and, with a rough, deep voice he said in pidgin English, '*Padi e, wettin deyhappen now? Why you come stone-face like this? [37]*'

'*Na big problem o, padi! No be say my face sad only, my case sef dey bad! [38]*' Francis replied, also in pidgin English.

Francis then told him how he had dropped out, with the conclusion that Harry was the cause of his plight.

Actually, Francis had been lusting after a young beautiful lady. The lady was studying in the same department as Francis – the Department of Mass Communication, although he was two years ahead of her. Francis, being a very shy man, was unable to approach her and it had made him sick. He had only admired

---

37 Hey friend, what's the matter? Why is your look so sad?
38 It's a big problem, friend! It's not only that my face looks sad, but my case itself is bad!

her beauty each time he saw her but could not approach her. However, the young lady was not aware of this – in fact, she did not know Francis and so was unaware of the fact that she was being desired, even this much, by this lustful young man.

Francis had wanted to give up on the young lady and concentrate on his studies since he was too shy to approach her but for his friend Harry, who had spurred him on. But then, Francis had not been emotionally stable on the issue; and together with some other more serious and emotionally disturbing issues, he had been unable to cope with his studies. But unfortunately he had only kept on hoping things would improve, until he ended up dropping out of school altogether. He therefore accused Harry of being responsible for his failures.

'And is that why you are so dejected as if you are a girl?' chuckled Harry. 'That's no big deal. Come on, cheer up! Be a man; life keeps going on! That's just it!'

'What is this you're saying, Harry?' exclaimed Francis. 'I should keep on bubbling when I dropped out of school?!'

'Hell, you think you are the only dropout in the whole world?' continued Harry. 'Dropping out of school is not the end of the world. That's just it! Look, did you hear of the rape of six girls on this campus four days ago?'

'Of course, I heard. And the rapists were expelled – who on this campus won't hear such news? Uh-huh, what about that? What has that got to do with the matter on ground?'

'Now listen, Francis,' replied Harry in a deep and low voice, 'if you must know and if I must tell you –' He paused and cleared his throat. 'I', he continued, 'was one of the rapists who has now been expelled from this campus!'

'Huh!' exclaimed Francis.

'That's just it! To show you you ain't the only one in a situation,' finished Harry. 'What do you want to do now?' he asked.

'Me? I am going home…back to my town – Ikaodọgba town… find some petty job…or, no – I just don't know!'

'Look, let me lend you a bit of my common sense. If you go back home, damn it, you lose the two mice you're chasing – you lose in two ways!'

'What do you mean?'

'Okay. You've lost your academics now, uh? You wanna lose her too?'

'Her?' queried a puzzled Francis. 'Who is her?'

'Her! The girl you are dying for, man!' replied Harry. 'I advise you to enjoy her and then go back to your town –mission accomplished!'

'To be frank with you, Harry, I cannot understand your nonsensical, inane ideation these days! Complete idiocy! Complete absurdity!' shouted an infuriated Francis.

'Hey! *Efiko*[39]! ' Harry hailed him.

'In any case,' added Francis, 'how possible is this?'

Harry paused a bit. Then instantly, he got an idea.

'O boy! It is possible! I'll tell you how. You see, you're *efiko*; and I've found out that the babe too likes her book too much!'

'And what about that?' interrupted Francis.

'I tell you, man, it's a sure bet if you wanna get her!'

'What?

'Her academics! Through her academics.'

'How?'

'Good! Now, you see, she can do anything for "book" – she can even marry you, if that's what you want!'

Francis chuckled.

---

39 Slang that means bookworm.

'Now, you'll just pretend to be interested in her studies,' Harry went on. 'That's just it! But don't tell her you've dropped out o! Because you may be so honest to tell her that!'

'*Haba*[40]! What kind of person d'you take me for?' Francis chuckled.

'A girl! A shy girl – that's who you are!' teased Harry.

They both laughed.

'As I was saying,' continued Harry, 'you gonna give her the impression you're in your final year; and you'll begin to help her with her work, and gradually become closer and closer to her till'

They laughed.

Harry saw someone coming towards the main gate, around where they stood. When the person could be seen clearly and recognised, Harry alerted Francis.

'Hey, look! Here she comes!' he exclaimed.

The person was a tall, slender young lady. She was dark in complexion and beautiful. She was beautifully dressed in a white pleated skirt and a cream blouse. She had on a pair of silvery hoop earrings and a pair of black strappy sandals on her feet. Her hair was plaited in cornrows. The lady is not unfamiliar to us: for this is twenty-three year old Romoke Bayetiri!

'What an opportunity!' exclaimed an excited Harry. 'Now, come on, go and meet her. Hey, go right away!'

'N... No – Wait – Not now,' hesitated Francis; 'you see, it's too impromptu.'

'What the hell, come on! Loo... look at you. Too girlish!' remarked Harry.

'Thank you. Leave me. Thank you,' replied Francis.

Romoke passed by and entered through the campus gate as Francis surveyed her at a distance, from head to toe, with his

---

40 Come on!

lustful eyes.

'And so, I'll see you later, Francis,' said Harry, about to leave.

'Okay,' replied Francis; 'thanks for your clever strategies. You see, I'll follow them all.'

'I trust you!' replied Harry. '*Hey, padi mi, you go give me sometin now – my so-so talk no be for free now!* [41]' Harry said in pidgin English.

Francis put his hand into his pocket and brought out a naira note.

'Take! *Everytin' na so-so "wettin you go give me, wettin you go give me"!* [42]' Francis said casually.

'*Fransi, Franko!*' Harry hailed him as he collected the money.

'*Na me be that o!* [43]' Francis replied jokingly as they parted.

Francis then headed for his apartment off-campus.

* * *

The daylight elapsed, giving way to nightfall. The lectures for the day had come to a close. Students were returning from the lecture theatres and from the library. However, some were just going to the library for a quiet study as the twilight brought relief from the scorching African sun. As darkness fell, the campus street lights came on. You could see silhouettes of boys and girls in cute boy-girl pairs –boys and girls loitering in the glow of the street lights, cooing romantic words to each other.

Three weeks had passed since Francis and Harry discussed about Romoke; and Francis had approached her as Harry had advised him to.

And now, in Romoke's room in the hostel, she sat on her

---

41 Hey friend, you have to give me something - I shouldn't talk for this long for no pay!
42 You always demand for money for every help offered!
43 That's me.

bunk bed, talking to her bunk mate. Romoke's bunk mate, Omolara, a 25 year old, who had been brought up by her grandmother in the village until her early teens, was in her fourth year. She was a lady of twenty-five. She grew up with her grandmother in the village till her early teen. Romoke had at one time taken her to her village and Romoke's mother urged Omolara to take care of her 'younger sister', as she put it, when she discovered what a responsible girl Omolara was.

'I see you moving with Francis Alantakun these days,' said Omolara, discussing with Romoke – 'I hope he is just a friend.'

'Ah, Omolara, he's just a friend; he's just helping me with my academics,' explained Romoke – 'but do you know him, or what?'

'I know him,' replied Omolara.

'How much do you know about him?' enquired Romoke. 'Is he good? I mean, is he academically good?'

'Erm, yes, I should think so,' replied Omolara; 'because – I can remember – when I was in my Year One and he also was in Year One then, he won an award for the school in an international competition in Mass Communication. Our school came second overall. He's a scholarly student.'

'Wow! okay, is it true he's studying Mass Communication also, and that he is in his final year? Why? Because, I just don't know, I'm somehow suspicious,' enquired Romoke.

'Yes, he is studying Mass Communication', replied Omolara, 'and he should be in his final year, now – he is in his final year.'

'If that's the case,' remarked Romoke, 'I'm quite lucky that he's helping me with my academics – I'm so lucky.'

'But Romoke, I have reservations about you taking him as a close friend,' said Omolara.

'Reservations?'

'Yes.'

'What reservations and why?'

'He's – should I say – he's somehow loose with ladies. I just don't like his relation with ladies; and I won't want your friendship with him to end in tears – you know, a sheep that befriends a dog will one day eat dirt, as the elders say.'

'What do you mean by "being loose with ladies"? Is he promiscuous?'

'Erm, I don't think so.'

'Okay, has his relationship with any lady been sexual, or what?'

'I can't really say; but the crab, the elders say, watches over its head with its eyes.'

'If you don't know then, and you can't tell precisely, why not keep quiet instead of being unnecessarily envious!' shouted Romoke.

'What do you mean?' Omolara queried, her expression suddenly changing. 'Are you calling me an envious liar?'

'You have said it yourself – I didn't call you that!' Romoke replied with an angry tone.

'Wait a minute, what's come over you, Romoke?' said Omolara.

'Nothing! Absolutely nothing!' replied Romoke angrily.

At this point of the verbal contention, Cynthia, another room mate and friend of Romoke, came into the room, smartly dressed in a black and white trouser suit. She was a been-to lady of twenty, and she had a sing-song accent.

'What's up girls?' she said.

'Oh Cynthia! You're back,' replied Omolara. 'How has your day been?'

'Oh,fantastic!' replied Cynthia. 'and yours?'

'We thank God,' replied Omolara.

'Oh, sweetheart, how're you doing?' Cynthia said to

Romoke.

'I'm fine, thanks,' she replied.

There was an awkward pause.

'What's up?' Cynthia said, breaking the silence. 'I think I heard you arguing as I came in?'

'Oh, it's nothing,' said Omolara.

'All right then,' said Cynthia.

She was about to get into bed when she remembered something.'Oh! I almost forgot – Romoke, I met er, Francis on my way back. He asked me to tell you that er, that he's still working on your class assignment and that by tomorrow – 3 p.m tomorrow afternoon, you should meet him in the library. He said by then he'd have been through with it and er, he's gonna explain 'em all to you'

'Thank's so much,' said Romoke.

'My pleasure dear,' replied Cynthia. 'Romoke, you are lucky, you know?' she added. 'That guy, your pal, is quite studious. You know what? He'd once won the school an international competition award - you're, in fact, so lucky!.

'Oh thank you,' replied Romoke.

'And', Cynthia added in a low voice and with a sensuous tone, 'he's such a gorgeous guy, you know!'

'Meaning?' queried Romoke.

'Meaning that somebody can't just help eyeing him up!' Cynthia chuckled.

'Ah, your have a dirty mind, Cynthia!' commented Romoke.'It's stained with dirty thoughts!'

'Dirty? Oh well you can give me some soap flakes to wash it out then. – I don't think mine will be sufficient enough for such mental cleansing!' Cynthia joked.

Omolara chortled with amusement.

'Oh, I'm afraid, I've got no soap flakes – I don't use them.

Do you mind using my soda?' Romoke asked jokingly, offering her a bar of soap.

Omolara chortled again at the drama,

'Wow! What is this!?'exclaimed Cynthia, looking at the bar of soda rather strangely.

'Have you never seen soda in your life? Or what's so strange about this?' said Romoke mockingly. 'This is what we use for laundry in the village – rural "detergent", o!'

'Then if that's the case,' Cynthia concluded jokingly, 'I'd rather not wash off my dirt than wash with soda!'

'Then you must be a daughter to the Biblical Naaman!' remarked Romoke.

'Whatever!' Cynthia said in a sing-song.

They all laughed at the joke – so much so that Romoke and Omolara forgot their earlier argument.

* * *

About half past four one Sunday evening; Romoke came to the front of a bungalow. On the gable of it there was a sign written with bold lettering 'BIG BOYZ VILLA' and on the walls were different posters pasted: 'JAZZ NITE...'; 'VOTE... AS STUDENTS' UNION PRESIDENT...'; 'MISS UniIjesha BEAUTY CONTEST...' and the like. From all these, you could tell that the house was inhabited by students – (students of the University of Ijesha).

Romoke's friendship with Francis was then two months old. She had come to visit Francis at home for this is where he lived. She needed him to go through some of her school work as she had a very important test in one of her compulsory courses the next morning. So, he had given her an appointment for half past four, that day.

Romoke entered the house and walked along the corridor. The house was unduly silent because Francis was the only one in.

He invited her into his room.

Without further delay, the lesson started as Francis taught her with erudition. They sat on the bed, while the books were placed on a stool in front of them. Romoke was enjoying the tuition as well as the company of a lively Francis.

It was now quarter past eight in the evening and really quite dark outside; however they still had a lot of ground to cover as they had spent a lot of the time kidding around. Francis gave Romoke some exercises to work through.

Francis went out of the room. By the time he came back he was only wearing a pair of boxer shorts and a vest. He shut the door behind him and sat down on the bed right beside Romoke. He placed his hand sensuously on her lap. Romoke looked up quickly and their eyes met. Francis opened his mouth and the first words that came out of his lips were: 'I love you'. Then there followed an utterance of carefully ordered romantic praise as he spoke softly and sweetly. The voice that issued those words was as sweet as the fragrance of spring flowers under the soft radiance of the sun. His words flowed out easily like extra virgin olive oil poured out of an alabaster jar. His breath was as fresh as the dawn when the dew wets the green grass; while his smile was sexy, charming, enchanting, captivating, and his eyes, like twin stars, twinkled in his dark face.

Romoke was caught in the web of his charm. Francis' words were so sweet that soon Romoke forgot her bitter past. His gentle caress on her lap was like a terminal from which an impulse so strong surged and which produced in her an electricity of sexual desire. She was so captivated by his bare, gorgeous physique, and by his irresistible passionate words, that her tendency towards having sex, which had been lying asleep all this while, was aroused – and before Romoke knew it, alas, they were in bed together.

* * *

Romoke arrived at her class the following morning for the test. But she was fifteen minutes late and the test had already begun. She greeted the lecturer conducting the test. 'Good morning sir.'

'Good morning,' replied the lecturer. 'Can I help you?' he queried.

'I am here for the test sir,' she answered.

'Really? That's great, for you to be coming this early!' the lecturer said sarcastically; and the class burst into giggles.

'Shush! You're having a test!' he stilled the class, and then he turned to Romoke again. 'By the way, were you not aware of the time for the test? Will you answer me!'

'I'm sorry sir,' Romoke apologised, bending her knees briskly.

'Oh, I see! You've really burned the midnight oil – you look like you have not slept!' the lecturer remarked.

He gave her her test paper.

'You have roughly forty-five minutes to go,' he said.

For the first ten minutes that Romoke sat down, she could not put down anything. It appeared as if all that Francis had taught her had been 'deleted' from her brain.

When she saw that it was difficult for her to 'retrieve' them, she thought of an alternative – "*expo*" – or more formally, exam malpractice!

Oh my God, I can't remember what Francis taught me. What a fool I am! What a big fool! I have gained nothing in the long run. He succeeded in using me, while I am left empty-headed! But no, I can still do something – there should be some smart guys here.

She saw a young man sitting at the back, a few seats away from her. She knew he was quite good so she tried to get his attention, and when she could, she communicated to him through gestures, asking him to help her with some questions.

When the young man agreed, she crouched low and moved deftly to him, and got a rough piece of paper containing the answers to the questions from him. She squeezed it into a tiny mass and thrust it into her brassière. Then again in a crouch, she moved deftly back to her seat, and then brought out the piece of paper, fondly called among students '*expo*' or '*orijo*'. She started copying down the answers– Everything was done so quickly, so much so that the supervising lecturer didn't notice anything.

When it was ten minutes to the end of the test, the lecturer announced this to the class. Romoke hastened up. All her five senses were at work. As she was mindful to write the correct thing so also was she alert and sensitive lest the lecturer noticed her cheating.

'Pens up! Submit!' ordered the lecturer. 'I'll count one to seven: if by seven, you haven't submitted your script, then "mark it yourself"!'

Romoke hastened to finish her work, sweating profusely. At last, she finished and she submitted.

'… Six –' the lecturer rounded off the counting – 'and Seven! Good morning once again.' And with that, he walked out with the scripts.

* * *

One early Monday morning, two weeks after Romoke's test, Francis was in his room with a nineteen year old girl in bed with him

A hard knock was heard on the door.

'Yes, who's that?' queried Francis.

The person at the door opened the door and entered, and lo, it was Romoke!

'Romoke! What's it?' asked a surprised Francis. 'Why have you come so early? I hope there's no problem.'

Romoke did not respond for a while but she looked very upset. Then after a while she spoke. 'Can I see you outside?' she requested in a low voice.

'Okay, let's go outside,' said Francis, getting up.

'To where, Francis?' the girl flared. 'You can't leave me here to attend to another girl! Let her say whatever she has to say here; or else, let her be silent forever!' she shouted.

'Sweet virgin bride, I dare not put any impediment to your matrimony with Francis!' Romoke said sarcastically with a deep voice and then hissed and walked out.

Francis ran after her. What is the problem? Why are you being so sarcastic?' he said. '*Haba*, that was way too much! Anyway, why do you want to see me? – is something the matter? I hope there's no problem?'

Romoke did not reply. When they got outside, they stood under a tree at a place hidden from public view.

'Now talk to me Romoke; what is wrong?' asked a worried Francis.

Romoke unfolded a sheet of paper that contained some information to him.'The result of the test,' she said.

'The result of the test?' asked Francis rather anxiously. 'Is it good? Did you pass? What was your grade? I hope you didn't fail? Come on, tell me!'

Romoke did not respond, but the look on her face suggested that there was a problem.

Francis hurriedly snatched the sheet of paper from her hand and stared at it anxiously.'But… but wait a moment,what is this? I mean, this doesn't look like a test result?'

'Is that so?'

'Yes, this looks like a medical report. "Both urine and serum beta HCG levels were diagnostic of…" Oh, what's all this? I don't even understand the medical jargon!'

'Who said anything about the academic test in the first

place? That's the result of the test I went for at the campus medical centre very early this morning, when I was vomiting.'

'You did not tell me that you are ill. How are you feeling now? Is it malaria or what?'

Romoke did not answer.

'In any case,' continued Francis, 'what's my own palava? What concerns me in this that you now bring the result of your malaria-or-whatever test to me?'

'If you can't understand what's there, I think I should tell you, or else you won't stop your nonsense talk!' said Romoke, cutting in.

'And what is there?' asked Francis.

'The summary of everything you are seeing there is that I am a few weeks pregnant!' replied Romoke.

'What? pregnant? For who?'

'Ha! What a question! For you, of course!'

'You can't be serious! Romoke, please tell me you're joking!'

'You better accept the reality of it now and let's start planning for how to take care of the baby.'

'Huh? Take care of what? Ah! I'm not ready to be a father yet. No, I'm not.'

'And what is that supposed to mean?'

'It simply means, erm – it simply means we should find a way of... I mean – of getting rid of it!'

'Huh? Of doing what?'

Francis looked into her eyes then spoke gently.

'You see, Romoke, you just have to do it; you know you can't continue your studies with this pregnancy, especially when you become heavy. You see, to terminate it will not require you to go to one hospital or the other– I'll just get some pills for you and you'll use it – it is very safe, no danger; but, you see, the earlier, the better. Now that the foetus is still only one little thing, and now that it's still safe, let's get rid of it!'

Romoke became lost in thought for a while. For a moment, scenes and voices in her past were replayed in her mind. The scene of her throwing away her baby came to mind. She remembered how she waved at her baby and bade him farewell forever; and that was indeed the last time she had seen him! The words of her mother echoed in her mind: Once bitten, twice shy: beware of recurrence of evil... Do not allow anyone to ruin you again....

'Mm, I handed the first to wild animals to kill: will I still murder this one?'she mused.

'Pardon?'

'I wasn't speaking to you!'

'All right – and what's your decision? Do you agree to get rid of it and I'll get the pills for you right away?'

'NO! I am not aborting my baby!' Romoke objected firmly.

'Then in that case, I'm not the father of the baby!' replied Francis, walking away from her.

'What do you mean? Are you walking out on me, Francis?' gasped Romoke. 'You must be kidding!'

She seized him by his pyjamas top and held it firmly in her hands.

'Will you leave my clothes and don't make them rough! Silly girl!' shouted Francis.

'Uh? What did you just call me?' shouted Romoke.'Me – silly girl?'

'Leave my clothes, or I'll teach you sense!' shouted Francis again.

'Do what you want to do! This pregnancy belongs to you and I'm not aborting it; if you like, kill me – irresponsible man!'

'Uh? Me?'

He spread his palm wide and slapped her with some force.

Romoke yelled as she fell against the tree, releasing her grip on Francis' shirt. 'But you said you love me – is this how you love me? Francis, you tricked me! You used me! You son of the devil! It is God that will punish you! You will not escape! You wolf in sheep's clothing! Son of a bitch! God will punish you! God will punish you! Son of the devil!!' she shouted amidst tears.

Francis hissed and turned to go in but stopped abruptly and turned around again to tell her once more of his unchanging stand.

'Look, Romoke, if you love yourself, agree to get rid of the pregnancy. This isn't murder. The thing inside there is just a clot of blood – just a developing embryo that has no feelings. The longer you wait in deciding, the more risky it will be. If you make up your mind today, I'll hand the pills to you in less than five minutes. Romoke, the earlier you terminate it, the better for your dear life; the longer you delay, the more risky it will be for you! When you make up your mind to do it, then you can come to me!' And then he walked out, leaving Romoke, whose mouth was wide open, outside.

'Goodness me!' she exclaimed.

She stood up from the ground and stood there, just staring into space. Omolara's words of caution were replaying in her mind" ...I just don't like his relation with ladies; and I will not want your friendship with him to end in tears.... The crab, the elders say, watches over its head with its eyes!"

'Ah,' Romoke exclaimed, 'I'm a fool!'

* * *

As days and weeks passed, Romoke was becoming less and less cheerful and lively. Her roommates noticed her mood; but when they asked her, she told them that her low mood was due to her experiencing symptoms of malaria so that when they saw her vomiting due to the pregnancy, they would think it was due to malaria.

Romoke was falling behind in her academics and missing lectures became a habit. She was close to her head of department, Dr. Emeka. The man had developed an interest in her and related with her as his daughter. Romoke used to go to his office to greet him often, and used to stay with him in his office at her leisure. But since she knew that she was pregnant, she stopped going there lest he discover. However, Dr. Emeka, was a man with a very busy schedule and did not ask after his 'daughter'. He was too busy to find out why Romoke had not come to visit him in his office as she normally would. *She is probably busy with various tests that is why she has not come lately. I am sure nothing is wrong and she will most likely come after her tests he thought.*

Now Romoke was sitting in the library with books in front of her. She wanted to read, but she could not. Her mind was so disturbed and she was confused.

Hmm, I made myself cheap. But how was I so foolish to quickly forget my bitter past by his mere sweet talk and be lured? Ah, what should I do now?

'Hmm, see my life!' she sighed.

Romoke looked up as though trying to receive direction from above. She became lost in thoughts. She then seemed to hear Francis' words again in her mind's ears: Romoke, the earlier you terminate it, the better for your dear life; the longer you wait before terminating it, the more risky it will be for you! When you make up your mind to do it, then you can come to me! Then immediately after, her mother's solemn words took over: *...Some would come to entice you with sweet words – It is the person with a problem that will know how to go about the problem....*

'Mmm, what should I do?' she sighed. She packed her books and left for the hostel.

Romoke bore the burden in her mind alone. She couldn't tell anyone – not even her close friend Omolara; for she feared the shame, the ridicule, the contempt, the blame – and so on.

One day, Omolara called Romoke apart, having noticed her rather frequent vomiting and her spitting quite often, to verify in privacy whether she was pregnant. Omolara asked her questions in a gentle manner and came across as an understanding friend. Nonetheless, Romoke denied being pregnant and maintained that it was only malaria. Romoke immediately walked out from there, and Omolara shook her head in pity. *'Ẹni a wi fun, ọba je o gbọ; ẹni a sọrọfun, ọba jẹ ogba!* [44]' she said.

On a Friday morning, she sat down to think.

Where do I go from here? What do I do? Oh, look at me! His sweet words enticed me; I was flattered and fooled. Poor me!

She paused and went on.

But I think I will go to him. But what will I tell him?

'Mm, I know what I will tell him. I know what I will tell him,' she muttered as she got up.

* * *

Romoke arrived at Francis' house. Francis was outside with some of his house-mates; they were washing clothes, and were chatting as they washed.

Romoke greeted them.

'Can I see you, Francis?' she requested.

'Okay,' replied Francis – 'should we go inside?'

'Yes; that's fine,' she replied.

They went to his room.

---

44 (Yoruba saying) The person who is warned, may they hear; the person who is admonished, may they listen

Romoke looked Francis straight in the eyes. Then she spoke. 'Francis, why do you take pleasure in a callous attitude, as if the God of vengeance is not there in Heaven? In any case, my mind is made up – whatever you want to do, do – it can't be changed!'

Francis grew furious.

'Your mind is made up? I can't change it? Then go and give birth to your baby! Come on, go! Is it me that would be relieved of the pregnancy worry, or you – if you get rid of it? It doesn't take me five minutes to hand the pills to you if you are ready now! You're just making a mountain out of a mere mole hill! Just go!' he shouted.

'But are you not the one who said I should come when I've made up my mind?' Romoke replied with a changed tone. 'And that's why I've come. Now I have told you that I've made up my mind and that nothing can change it; so whatever you want to do, whatever you want to give me, you go on. And you now grow furious like a snake wanting to bite a butterfly!'

'Ha, I did not know that was what you meant!' said Francis, feeling awkward. 'I'm sorry,' he added. He paused and then went to his wardrobe. 'I have the pills here – I knew you'd come eventually,' he said, searching and searching. He saw it and offered it to her. 'There you go,' he said. 'I've had it for some time now – I always keep them. Now, should I get you a cup of water to take it?'

'Yes please,' replied Romoke.

He gave her a cup of water.

Romoke took the cup and just stared at the pills; for she was apprehensive.

'Come on, Romoke; take it; there'll be no problem – I can assure you,' he said encouragingly.

Romoke's hand was visibly shaking as she started to take the pills. She then closed her eyes firmly and put them in her mouth; but she couldn't take in the water to swallow them, for she feared.

'Take it, come on; take it,' he said.

She then drank the water and with it swallowed the pills, and then she shivered a bit.

'Don't worry; nothing bad will happen,' Francis said.

* * *

Romoke was leaning forward in the bathroom, in her hostel, vomiting; but what she was vomiting was blood! It was the afternoon of that Friday, and she had already vomited blood twice. Omolara was standing beside her. 'Easy, Romoke,' Omolara said. 'How are you feeling?'

As Romoke was about to answer, she suddenly felt like urinating. She immediately rushed to the toilet. Omolara followed her.

When she got to the toilet to urinate, lo and behold, she bled from her private parts, continuously; and she began to feel very weak.

When Omolara saw this, she, with a few other roommates – Cynthia inclusive – took her to the campus medical centre, but she was immediately referred to the campus teaching hospital and taken there.

* * *

Romoke was lying down on the hospital bed in the Gynaecology Ward, in Block 09 of the University of Ijesha Teaching Hospital in Ijesha town. She had just been rushed there, and a blood transfusion was started immediately because she had lost a lot of blood. She had also had some tests done earlier to check out the state of her internal organs especially her womb and the state of the baby.

Omolara and Cynthia sat by her bed, consoling her.

The medical doctor, Dr. Yakub, came to her side. He was a

tall, dark-complexioned man. He was dressed in a black pair of trousers and a light blue long-sleeved shirt, with a tie. He had on a pair of black shoes and he was holding a black stethoscope in his hand.

'How are you feeling, Romoke?' asked Dr. Yakub.

'Not better, Doctor,' she replied.

'Sorry dear,' Dr. Yakub consoled her. 'Friends, do you mind just excusing us for a couple of minutes?' said Dr. Yakub, turning to Omolara and Cynthia.

'No we don't mind,' they said as they stood up and left the ward, but they were rather anxious.

'Romoke, I want you to be courageous and take heart,' the doctor began. 'Everyone faces challenges in life,' he continued; 'but sometimes one challenge can lead to yet greater ones. When that happens, a person's attitude to the challenges determines, to a large extent, the person's victory.' He paused a bit. 'Romoke, a lady should not despair of life even if her womb would no longer be able to carry children!' he said, abruptly concluding.

Romoke sat up. 'I don't understand, Doctor,' she said anxiously; 'please tell me what's happening in clear terms – don't speak to me in riddles, please!' she begged.

'Relax, Romoke,' said the doctor; 'there's nothing to worry so much about.' He paused a bit. 'You're a big girl – I trust you should be able to contain yourself at an unpleasant report.'

'Unpleasant report!' exclaimed a troubled Romoke.

'Keep calm, Romoke,' said Dr. Yakub. 'Now, where did you get the pills you took to abort the pregnancy?' he asked.

'The guy that was responsible for the pregnancy gave me. Ah, wait a minute – he said he had had them for a long time! Ah!' Romoke said.

'Hmm! I thought as much!' said Dr. Yakub. 'Really, the drugs you took had expired; they caused a serious infection in your womb which resulted in severe damage to it. The result of the test we did shows multiple puncture wounds in your womb and we need to perform major surgery to remove it as soon as possible otherwise you could die.'

Romoke laid her two hands on her head and exclaimed, 'Yeh! My God!' and a tear rolled down her face.

'Come on, don't cry; nobody is without challenges. It's not the end of the world,' Dr. Yakub consoled her. 'Where are your parents residing?' he asked.

'In Ibupẹsọ,' replied Romoke as she wept.

'Where is that town? Is it also in this south-western part of the country?'

'Yes, sir.'

'Are your parents on the phone, so we can call them and inform them about your state and about the operation?'

'We live in the village, Doctor – Ibupẹsọ is a village; there are no telephones there. Besides, I'm from a poor family. My father is dead and only my mother is left to take care of me,' sobbed Romoke.

'I see!' he said. 'It's all right; stop crying, uh? Now, in that case, are you at all close to any member of staff of the institution, who may stand in for your parents in signing for the operation to be done, as we must perform the operation right away?' he enquired.

Romoke told him that she was close to her head of department, Dr. Emeka, who had taken her as his daughter and related to her as that. Romoke however did not have his telephone number. Dr. Yakub checked the telephone directory in his surgery which contained numbers of major offices in both the hospital and the institution. He looked through and found the phone number of the office of her head of department, Dr. Emeka. He called Omolara into his surgery to ask her a few questions.

Omolara sat facing Dr. Yakub. On his desk were

giant medical textbooks. On one end of the desk was a sphygmomannometer, and on the other end, a black analogue telephone.

He picked up the telephone receiver and dialled Dr. Emeka's office telephone number.

'Office of the head, Department of Mass Communication, the University of Ijesha. Good afternoon,' the secretary said at the other end.

'Good afternoon,' replied Dr. Yakub, 'Can I speak to the head of the department please?'

'Oh, yes. May I ask who is calling?'

'I'm Doctor Yakub from the University hospital.'

'All right. Just a minute, please.'

The secretary went to call Dr. Emeka and he took over the phone.

'Hello,' said Dr. Emeka.

'Hello sir,' replied Dr. Yakub. 'A young lady by the name Romoke Bayetiri is here presently in the University teaching hospital, at the Gynaecology ward, Block 09. We learnt that you are acquainted with her.'

'Yes – Romoke! What happened to her?!' exclaimed a worried Dr. Emeka.

'There's nothing to worry about sir; but we would quite appreciate it if you could find time to be here now, as we have to conduct a major surgery on her right away.'

'Eh! Is it that serious? All right, I'm coming right away.'

'Thank you.'

'All right.'

Twenty minutes later Dr. Emeka was there. He came down from his Peugeot 505 saloon car, a luxurious car in those days, and walked rather quickly to the Gynaecology Ward in Block 09.

He saw the doctor and they shook hands.

'Good afternoon, Doctor.'

'Good afternoon sir.'

'I was the one you spoke with on the phone some twenty minutes ago – Doctor Emeka.'

'Oh, you're welcome. Have your seat.'

They sat down and discussed. When Dr. Emeka learnt that Romoke had been pregnant and aborted it, he was furious.

'Goodness me!' exclaimed Dr. Emeka. 'What has come over her for goodness' sake? But who did she say is responsible for the pregnancy?'

'Actually, we didn't raise the issue of the boy responsible of the pregnancy, as this is not important now – she is about to face a major operation anytime from now as I told you on phone. You can always raise the issue after the operation.'

Before Dr. Yakub had set off for the operation, he encouraged Dr. Emeka.'Keep your mind at rest; there's no cause for alarm. The operation will be successful, by the grace of God,' he said – 'you just continue to beg God for her life,' he added.

Romoke was laid on a stretcher, to be wheeled into the theatre. Before she was wheeled in, Omolara stood by her side, and Romoke placed her hand in hers.

'I'm going into the theatre now,' Romoke said in a subdued voice: 'whether I will come out "wombless" or I will come out lifeless, my sister, I don't know!'

Omolara removed her hand from Romoke's hand and wiped a tear from her own eyes. Before she could return her hand, Romoke was wheeled away from there and into the theatre. The day was Friday, 29th May, 1981.

4

Depressed Again

On Saturday morning, the day following her operation, Romoke lay on the hospital bed with a blood drip needle passed into one of the veins of her left hand.

The nurses on the night duty were then handing over. The night duty nurses then left and the morning duty nurses resumed their work. Among the four nurses on duty that morning was a young lady, Chinyere. She had been on duty the afternoon of Friday when Romoke was brought in, and so she had seen her quite well, and she had also gone through her case note.

She went near Romoke and stood at her bedside. A tear was tricking down her closed eyes.

'Stop crying, sister,' Chinyere said.

She opened her eyes and looked at the nurse. Chinyere gave a warm smile. She drew the seat closer to her bed and sat.

'My sister,' she said, 'I have good news for you –it's this: There's still hope – yes, there's hope for you.'

Romoke did not respond, but in her mind she responded

with contempt. *There now! She just opens her mouth to say "There's still hope, there's still hope" –if she were in my shoes, she would hate to hear the cliché being trotted out to her!*

'I dreamt about you yesterday night,' Chinyere continued.

Romoke immediately sat up and wiped her tear. And she was attentive.

* * *

It seemed as though the wild animals in one particular jungle were full of fun. The birds were busy with singing their harmonious notes. The monkeys were engaged with acrobatic feats, jumping from one branch of a tree to another. The chatter of monkeys and the birds was exhilarating. And the squirrels proved expert climbers.

However, in this same jungle full of ecstatic and frolicsome animals a sad young lady stood, weeping dejectedly. She would not even be cheered by the fun of those animals, nor would be frightened by them or by their dreaded abode, the jungle.

The young lady was standing, with her head bowed, and laying her left hand on her belly over her womb, and in her right hand she was holding blood-stained swaddling clothes. She was weeping and lamenting. Then she raised her head – lo, we could see Romoke Bayetiri: and she cried with agony, 'Where are you, God? Where?'

Chinyere had been watching her from a distance all along, only shaking her head in pity. But when Romoke cried out, an extremely old Man who is known as The Ancient of Days, came to Chinyere and He said to her, 'Why do you stand just looking at sad Romoke? Go to her right now and say….'

* * *

'The Ancient of Days asked me to tell you this: "There is hope for your future; for not only will you be a mother again, but also, a grandmother",' Chinyere reported to Romoke on the hospital bed as she concluded the narration of her dream.

Thus did Chinyere deliver the message she had received for Romoke in her dream. She had finished narrating her dream to her and told her The Ancient of Days' exact words.

Romoke gave a chuckle of doubt. 'Is that ever possible? You're a nurse; you have medical knowledge – tell me how that is ever possible. I no longer have a womb; now you say that I will not only be a mother again, but also a grandmother!'

'I don't know,' replied Chinyere; 'but I do know that whatever way He chooses to fulfill His promise no one can question Him, for He is the Lord. And mind you, I never told you I said it; in fact, I don't fully understand this that The Ancient of Days said about you but I know you will: however I am sure that the Almighty who told me this has never for once lied, and He will not start telling a lie with your own matter, my sister!'

* * *

It was the afternoon of Sunday, the thirty-first of May,1981. Romoke had just been discharged from the hospital. She stood for quite a while in the exit doorway of the hospital as though hesitating to go on into her future and face the bleak outlook.

Romoke had changed pretty much in appearance. Anyone that knew her before she took those pills which damaged her womb and before she was operated upon and who now saw her as she left the hospital might readily take her for another person. She looked very pale and gaunt. Anyone that had known her earlier and now saw her by this time would pity her. What a life full of hurts, tears and costly failures hers was! For her, life was unfriendly, cruel and pitiless. She was now without a womb. It seemed to her like her whole world had come to an end.

When she left the hospital, she went to her hostel; and when she had rested a bit, she went to Francis' house. But then Francis, on hearing the rumour of Romoke's bleeding and operation on that Friday afternoon that the incident happened, and knowing that he might be looked for and arrested, had packed his belongings, waved his co-dwellers goodbye and boarded a public bus to his town, Ikaodǫgba. When she got to Francis' house, she was shocked at what she heard.

'Good afternoon. Please, is Francis at home?' she enquired from his co-dwellers in the corridor.

'Oh, Francis! He's not home; he's travelled!' replied Kenneth, one of the neighbours.

'Travelled!' said Romoke, surprised. 'To where?'

'To his town,' replied Badmus.

'Where's his town?'

'No one knows!' replied Badmus.

'Oh my goodness!' Romoke gasped. 'Please, when did he travel and when is he likely to return?'

'He travelled the day before yesterday and I doubt if he'll come back cos the guy packed all his loads!' replied Benson.

'Will he not be coming back to take his semester exams, or what?'

'Goodness! Ha-ha! The guy's no more a student, don't you know? He's dropped out since last year!' replied Badmus.

'What!?' Romoke gasped.

'Come on, Badmus! *Ya mouth no dey keep secret!*[45] ' reproved Kenneth.

'*Wettin now? No dey vex me dis afternoon a' beg!*[46]' said Badmus.

'What's the essence of the secret anymore, in any case?' Benson put in.

Romoke stood there shocked to her bones and it all seemed like a dream to her. She turned around dreamily and makes towards the door without even saying a word.

---

45 (Pidgin English) Your mouth can't keep a secret!
46 (Pidgin English) What now? please don't annoy me this afternoon.

'Would you want to leave a message just in case he comes to say hello?' teased Kenneth.

'It's not necessary,' she replied in a murmur as she went out.

She stood outside and stared into space, confused. Then suddenly an idea dropped in her spirit.

'I know what I will do. Yes, the chemist's!' she muttered to herself and grinned, and then moved on.

They watched her as she went out; and when she was too far to hear them, they laughed at her and made various caustic remarks about her.

* * *

Romoke got to her hostel and told Omolara that she was going home. Omolara was somewhat surprised at such a sudden decision to travel to her village, seeing that she had just gone through a major operation and would need much rest. Romoke however insisted on going home, giving the excuse that she was actually going home to have enough rest, which might not be possible on campus. At Romoke's insistence, she agreed. Omolara would have accompanied her home if not for an early morning test that she had got slated for the following day, Monday. Cynthia too would have followed Romoke in her place, but she wasn't around in the hostel then and Omolara didn't know when she would be back. However, Omolara implored Romoke to take good care of herself.

Romoke packed virtually all her belongings. Omolara was surprised to see this. She asked her why. Romoke's reply was that most of them were what she was not using frequently and which was better to be taken home; and also that she might need some of them at home during her pretty brief period of rest at home.

Omolara saw her off to the bus station, helping her carry the load. They got there and Romoke said to her, 'Let me release you now Omolara, so you can go and prepare for your test. I really appreciate all your friendly care and love. I wish I know how best I can pay back. Thank you very much, Omolara.'

'Oh not at all. My pleasure, dear,' replied Omolara. 'Aw, but what is this you're saying?' she said at once. 'Why this thank you now? Are you sure you're okay, Romoke?'

'I'm okay,' she replied. 'I'm all right, Omolara.'

'Are you sure?'

'Why, I'm sure!'

'All right.'

Omolara then waved her goodbye and left.

Romoke left her load at the bus station and walked down that street to a little chemist's which was in a rather secluded area. The chemist was an elderly man of about sixty.

'Good afternoon,' said Romoke.

'Good afternoon. You're welcome,' replied the chemist.

'Do you have – erm – poison?'

'Eh? What d'you call it? Poison! We don't sell poison here o!'

'Please, I can pay whatever amount you ask me to pay – just sell it to me!' begged Romoke.

'Please customer, don't put me into trouble,' shouted the chemist. 'Don't you stay in the country, or don't you listen to the news? Haven't you heard that the Federal Government has banned the sale of poisons these days? And they have sent out the police to arrest those that are still selling it – who even knows whether you are a secret police?' he commented as he eyed her and turned away.

'No, I'm not at all!' replied Romoke.

'So they always say!' the chemist chuckled. 'Look, the Prince of this world comes and finds nothing in me!' he said, mimicking Jesus Christ's statement when he was nearing his crucifixion.

'I'm not a secret police, I swear to God!' replied Romoke.'And I'm not using the poison on anybody; I'd take it myself.'

'Ha! Young lady, why?'exclaimed the startled chemist.

'Baba, I'm tired of life,' replied Romoke –'if life's not worth living, death should be worth dying, I think.'

'Ah,young lady, don't say that!' reproved the chemist. 'You're too young and too beautiful to be thinking of killing yourself. Some old people like me on their deathbed in the hospital, are begging God to even extend their life span, even if it is by only twenty-four hours more!'

'Please, Baba, I beg you in the name of all that is good, sell this thing to me!'begged Romoke.'I know you have it. Please Baba, do this for me, I beg you!'

The chemist looked on awhile,and then suddenly he turned and headed for his store. He stopped abruptly and turned around to Romoke. 'Can you recognise it when you see it?' he asked.

Romoke wondered at such a question. 'What type of question is that?' she said. 'Don't you know it yourself?'

'I just wanted to know if you know what you want to buy, so you can choose the best; cos there are the effective ones and there are ones that are painfully slow at work,' explained the chemist.

'OK – I can't recognise it when I see it, but help me get the good one, please,' requested Romoke.

The chemist entered into his stores. He stayed quite a long while there, and then finally came out with a black polythene bag. He stood behind the counter and put the polythene bag on it. He brought out a medicine jar with a printed label that told that it was poison. Bringing out the poison, the man said, 'I got the good one for you; it is fifty-three naira – no more, no less!' This was a considerable sum in those days when naira had much value.

'Ha, Baba! Come on, that's much too much! Are you

joking? It can nearly pay my school fees!'

'Lady, I'm not joking! You know I shouldn't be selling this; so you shouldn't even have the gut to question my price – you know?' the chemist replied. 'Fifty-three naira – no more, no less!' he reiterated.

'All right, Baba; give it to me,' said Romoke.

The chemist returned the poison jar into the polythene bag and Romoke almost emptied her purse to pay. He collected the money from her and then after gave the polythene bag to her and she left. He fixed his eyes on Romoke as she walked out. He rested his jaw on his palm and his elbow on the counter, gazing at her and shaking his head in pity of the poor soul.

* * *

Omolara got back to the campus to hear that her Continuous Assessment test that was scheduled to hold the early morning of the following day had been postponed to Wednesday morning that week. When she got to the hostel she told Cynthia who had then returned. 'Take your things, Cynthia; I think we can now leave for Ibupẹsọ!' she said.

'We might even meet Romoke at the bus station,' Cynthia said as she packed her things.

'Of course – but that's if we're fast enough,' Omolara replied.

'Wow, an adventure to the village!' exclaimed an excited Cynthia.

'Come on, we're not going for an adventure; we're only going to see to it that Romoke gets home safely! I know you love pleasure and leisure!' she joked.

'Oh yah, those are my treasures!' replied Cynthia. 'But yours are pressures, full measure!' she joked.

Omolara laughed. 'Come on, be serious; you've come again with your jokes – you've forgotten we're in a hurry.'

They packed their few things into a single bag each and left. When they got to the bus station they learnt that Romoke's bus had just left not more than ten minutes earlier. But although she had just left, they still decided to travel to Ibupẹsọ to know her welfare. They had also taken along beverages and multivitamins to give to her as they didn't give her anything when she left. Before long thier bus was ready to go and then it got on the road.

* * *

Romoke's bus had journeyed far. The bus was heading for Odo-Akan town. Out of the seventeen-kilometre-long journey, it had then covered about ten kilometres. Romoke, when the bus would eventually stop at Odo-Akan, a neighbouring town to her village Ibupẹsọ, was to trek the one-kilometre-long pathway to Ibupẹsọ.

Now, Romoke was sitting at the rear of the speeding bus. They had got to a village called Itakuje. There was still about seven kilometres to go. She looked at the village which was off the road on which they journeyed. She asked the driver to stop for her there. The bus stopped and she came down with her loads.

While the bus was about starting, a young man of about thirty, who was dressed in *buba*[47] and *ṣọọrọ*[48] and who had tribal marks on his cheeks was looking carefully at Romoke. *This should be Romoke... No, I think it only looks like – this person is very pale and lean.*

Romoke was moving bit by bit with her loads. The bus started, and Romoke looked back at it. Seeing Romoke's face and recognising her, the young man said to himself, *Aha, it's Romoke!* And the bus zoomed off.

Romoke trekked a little farther but would not go so far for the village was just at a stone's throw from her. She tried

---

47 A simple top
48 A simple pair of trousers

carrying her loads into a bush. When she had carried everything there and she was there in the bush, she opened one of her bags and brought out the black polythene bag. She took out the poison jar from it and a piece of paper flew out with it the polythene bag.

'This Pharmacist put a note there?' she muttered. 'I guess what is there is nothing but words of persuasion for me to forbear to commit suicide – but it is a lie; nobody can change my mind; it's made up!'

Romoke would read the content of the piece of paper but immediately she refused to, as she thought the encouragement of the words might be so strong that it would persuade her to forbear to attempt suicide; for she had made up her mind to end her life. She however said she was going to read the content of the note after she had taken the poison, when nothing could change her suicide act again! She was that resolute!

As she returned the pieces of paper into the polythene bag, she saw another thing – the exact money she paid for purchasing the poison, inside the nylon bag, returned to her! She laughed. 'Ha! Ha! All these aren't enough to stop me!' Ah, alas, alas! Romoke was resolute to die, what then could stop her?

Then she looked straight ahead of her and spoke as though addressing someone. Her tone freely bespoke a hurt so unspeakable and she cried with all the bitterness in her soul.

'Francis, I hate you! My soul curses you, Francis Alantakun! My womb curses you! My foetus which your pills killed, curses you!'

She did a whole lot of talking and talking, wanting to pour out her hurt and bitterness raw as though to listening bush.

But then while she was there talking and cursing, a little girl of eight came into the bush to pass excrement. In villages like this in those days, there were no toilets – if there were any at all, it was usually one or two pit latrines to serve the entire village. So the bush was usually the toilet!

The little girl was about rolling up her dress and squatting when she heard someone's voice in the bush, the person seeming to be talking and laughing to no one in particular. She peered at the person through the spaces between the thickets. She saw a young lady, stony-faced and with a resolute look. She saw her holding the jar in her hand and talking to herself. Afraid, the girl immediately rushed out of the bush. It seemed to her as if the excrement had vanished in her bowels! All along, Romoke was not aware of the girl in the bush and her running out. Now, Romoke was already saying her last prayer.

The girl dashed out of the bush and ran. She ran past the frontage of a particular mud house, in front of which an old woman, in her late sixties, was sitting. The old woman's hair was grey with age and she wore it in plaits. Her face was wrinkled and she was slightly bent from old age. She had a few set of decaying teeth – they had been blackened by kola nuts. She had a set of tribal marks on her cheeks. And she held a long stick with the aid of which she walked, and in the other hand she held a woven *abẹbẹ*[49] with which she fanned herself as she relaxed.

'Come, Fadeke!' the old woman said, calling the girl back.

Fadeke stopped and went to her.

'*Eetiri, ọmọ mi?* [50]' she asked in Ọyọ dialect of Yoruba.

'*Mama Agba*, it is one lady in that bush where I wanted to do a poo,' replied Fadeke, pointed there.

'A lady?' said the old woman. 'How does she look? What did she do to you?'

'She's dressed in *oyinbo*[51] dress like those campus students; she has travelling bags beside her like someone coming from a journey; and she is there talking alone,' Fadeke tried to describe her. '*Mama Agba*, maybe she's a traveller and had run mad,' she guessed.

49 Hand fan
50 What happened my child?
51 Western

'What did she do to you?' asked the old woman.

'Nothing,' replied Fadeke; 'I think she didn't see me; but I was afraid when I saw her, that I can't even poo again.'

'All right, take me there,' the old woman said.

'Ah, me? No, I can't go there again – I'm afraid!' replied Fadeke.

'In that case,' said the old woman, 'wait here; stay with Funso for me – he's sleeping in the room – in case he wakes up.'

'All right, mama,' replied Fadeke.

The old woman was fondly called *Mama Agba*, a Yoruba phrase that literally means 'Elderly mother'. It was those in her neighbourhood that nicknamed her so, and for quite different reasons they did. 'She so much loved Funso her grandson, that you might think, if not for her age, that she is the mother rather than the grandmother – so the name *Mama Agba* suits her most,' some would say. 'She loves all the children in the neighbourhood and takes them as her children, hence she is *Mama Agba*,' some others would explain. 'She is a mother to us mothers in the neighbourhood; she relates with us as to her children; hence *Mama Agba* qualifies her most,' some mothers in the neighbourhood used to say.

Mama Agba walked with the aid of her staff, although slowly for her age, to the bush where Romoke was, leaving the sleeping five year old Funso to the care of Fadeke.

Romoke, where she was, was about to take the poison. She opened the jar and looked awhile into it. She sighed, and then looked up to the sky.

'*Ba'a mi* [52], I Romoke, your only daughter and child, am coming over there in a moment!' she said aloud. 'If life is not worth living, death should be worth dying!' she added.

She took the jar upand wanted to pour the content into the mouth, but she couldn't, as her hand quivered for fear.

---

52 Dad

'Be brave, Romoke; be brave!' she said. 'It is just once and for all – once and for all!'

* * *

At that same time in Romoke's house in Ibupęsọ, the man that had recognized Romoke when she had alighted from the bus was now sitting in the sitting room with Segilola. He had just told her how he saw Romoke, lean and pale, going towards Itakuje village. The man was also a villager in Ibupęsọ. Rotimi was his name.

'Rotimi, please tell me, are you sure it is Romoke you saw? I mean my Romoke?' asked worried Segilola.

'Yes, mama; my eyes were not deceiving me – I recognized her!' replied Rotimi.

Outside that old mud house, Omolara and Cynthia were approaching, walking at a slow pace. They were chatting as they walked.

'Is this the village? Bullshit!' said Cynthia.'Look, all messy. No street lights. I ain't yet seen'un house with electricity! Look, that 'un – see goat tied inside that house! Look, look – careful – messy fowl's dirt there! Oh damn, I thought the adventure's just gonna be fun. I still can't believe my eyes ain't seeing hallucinations, I swear!'

'Come on, keep all those comments to you, Cynthia,' reproved Omolara. 'There, we've got to Romoke's house! See it down there.'

They got to the door,knocked and entered.

'*Ẹkuule mama* [53],'Omolara greeted, bowing to touch one knee to the ground.

'*Kaabọ, ọmọ mi* [54],' replied Segilola. She turned to Cynthia. 'How are you, my dear?' she said.

53 A greeting used when you are entering a house that you went out from and you are part of or a house that you are quite acquainted with.
54 Welcome, my child.

'I'm fine, mama,' replied Cynthia, bending her knees briskly.

'Are you gone on break, or what; that you two have come to visit?' asked Segilola.

'No mama,' replied Omolara. 'Actually, we've come to visit Romoke and know her welfare,' she explained.

'Romoke! What happened to her?' exclaimed a worried Segilola.

'Oh, we thought she might have told you,' said Omolara.

'What? Please tell me; what happened to Romoke?' Segilola asked anxiously.

Omolara sensed that the mother had not known about Romoke's abortion story, and so she was careful about telling her the whole situation.

'Actually, mama, Romoke would tell you; we thought she has already told you,' replied Omolara.

'Please my daughters, I beg you by Ọṣun the goddess of children, tell me – *e o ni ri idamu ọmọ!* [55]' Segilola begged feelingly.

Omolara was moved. She looked up and looked down, not knowing what to do. Rotimi sat there looking intently at her; Segilola also stared at her, waiting anxiously to hear the next words about Romoke.

She took a breath to calm her down and then spoke. 'Mama, keep your mind at rest,' she said; 'it's nothing serious. She was just briefly taken ill and she'd got over it now.'

'Ha! Is it brief illness she had?' Cynthia cut in.'Let's tell the poor woman exactly what happened, for crying out loud!'

'Tell me *o jare* [56] ,'said Segilola, turning to Cynthia.

---

55 Your children will not cause you trouble!
56 Please

Omolara signalled with the eyes that Cynthia should not tell the woman. But then, Cynthia didn't understand the sign and thought some dirt had got into Omolara's eyes.

'Just a minute, let me be done with telling mama and I'll help you blow off the speck, uh?'

Omolara was somewhat disappointed.

'Now, mama,' began Cynthia, 'what happened was that Romoke was impregnated –'

'Huh!' exclaimed Segilola.

'She was impregnated; that's it,' continued Cynthia. 'She then took some pills to abort the pregnancy, and which badly damaged her womb–'

'Yeh!' exclaimed Segilola, laying her two hands on her head.

Omolara gently stepped on Cynthia's foot, signalling that she shouldn't continue any further. But alas, Cynthia's response was still embarrassing.

'What? Why stepping on me for goodness' sake?' she shouted.

'Go on,' Segilola said, beckoning to Cynthia.

'Erm – yah, her womb was badly damaged; so it had to be removed in a surgical operation,' Cynthia concluded.

'Ah! Ye gods! This is hard to swallow!' exclaimed Segilola. 'Where is she now?' she enquired.

Omolara opened her mouth in surprise as she sensed that Romoke hadn't arrived home. What a terrible moment! she said to herself. Then she replied, 'Ah, we ourselves thought she had arrived home! She left the campus before us just this afternoon; she told us she was going home!'

Segilola looked at Rotimi as he at the same time looked at her.

'Yeh! My head!' she exclaimed as she slowly sank on the

ground and fainted.

* * *

In that bush in Itakuje village, Romoke had just encouraged herself to take the poison; and then she felt so desperate, as resolute as never before. *Mama Agba* had already entered the bush and was nearing Romoke, although Romoke was unaware of her presence around. Romoke closed her eyes firmly. And then slowly… hm… slowly… she emptied the poison substance into her mouth and swallowed it. In less than three minutes after Romoke had poisoned herself, Mama Agba appeared, but alas, it was already too late! Romoke had swallowed the deadly substance! Alas, oh, alas!

'*Ee ṣe ọ, ọmọde 'ii?*[57] ' *Mama Agba* asked in a cool, soothing voice, in the Ọyọ dialect of Yoruba.

Romoke looked at her, shocked at first. Then she replied, 'Life challenges have made me to come to a point of despair of life, mama; and now I'm saying bye-bye to life!'

'Who is pursued by the *Eegun*[58] should persevere: as mortals grow tired, so also spirit beings grow tired!' the old woman remarked in a Yoruba proverb that is used to mean: 'Tough times never last but tough people do!' (In Yoruba land the religious masquerades are assumed to be spirits of ancestors.)

It was as though Romoke's eyes had just been opened, and the demon that had been motivating and spurring her to commit suicide, it seems, had left her to some solitary place, making jest of her, having succeeded in making her poison herself. Romoke's heart which had been resolute to commit suicide now melted like wax beside fire. She now regretted taking the poison and strongly wished she hadn't taken it. She laid her two hands on her head, weeping sorely. '*Mama*, I am a walking corpse! I am a lady who, though is still breathing, has already

---

57 What's the matter child?
58 Yourba traditinal masquerade.

had her obituary printed and got her death certificate issued!' she lamented.

Mama Agba did not understand the deeper meaning of her words. She only thought it was only out of being tired of life due to its attending problems that Romoke was saying all that. However, she kept on consoling her and urged her to come into her house with her loads.

Romoke carried her loads and *Mama Agba* helped her in carrying the lighter ones. She also took the poison jar; she put it back in the polythene bag and back into one of her travelling bags. They walked slowly out of the bush.

Mama Agba put her hand around her waist and led her gently, consoling her as they walked along. Romoke bit her forefinger. Tears ran down her eyes like water from an opened tap. She wept sorely, and in a matter of minutes she had exhausted her strength, so much that she had no more strength to weep; and then she started to groan.

And then they came to the house and she groaned with all her strength as they entered.

'God, show me mercy!!!'

5

Hope Again

'Now my dear, what is your name and what's the problem?' asked Mama Agba.

'Romoke is my name, mama – Romoke Bayetiri,' sobbed Romoke.

Romoke was sitting in Mama Agba's sitting room in Itakuje village that Sunday, the thirty-first of May, 1981. Mama Agba had just taken her in from inside the bush that she was when she took the deadly poison shortly before she got there. Now, Mama Agba had released Fadeke to go, who had stayed with five-year-old Funso, sleeping on a mat in the room; although Funso was not yet awake.

The sun was setting fast, and darkness was falling quickly. The rusty corrugated iron roofs of the mud houses were making their crackle, being cooled bit by bit. As the sunny afternoon gave way for a cool evening, little children started jumping out of their houses in the neighbourhood like nocturnal insects fly out of their crevices in the gathering gloom. The children played in the sand, their shout of fun pervading the cool evening.

Funso, sleeping in Mama Agba's room, was awoken by the happy noise made by these frolicsome children, his playmates. He jumped up from his mat and picked up his toy car. Now, the cart was hand-made from tins that had been beaten first into a flat shape and then dexterously shaped into the form of a vehicle. Village boys are usually dexterous in making such crafts which they use to keep themselves happy.

Funso took his cart and dashed into the sitting room. He saw Mama Agba; and on seeing the visitor Romoke with a sad look, he was at first stared back. Then he turned to Mama Agba. 'Mama, I want to go and play with my friends,' he said.

'All right, don't stay out late,' said Mama Agba; 'you come back before dark – OK?'

Funso nodded. He turned to go and then stopped abruptly and turned back. He looked at Romoke, and then smiled and stretched out his cart to her. 'Look, my motor! My friends made it for me!' he said.

The craft was an exquisite one with imitation of virtually every part of the body of a motor car.

Romoke, who had been weeping before, feigned a smile. 'It's fine – I like it,' she said.

'You didn't even greet our visitor, Funso, before showing her your toy,' Mama Agba reproved him. 'Now greet her as you should have done?'

He prostrated himself, greeting her.

'Get up – good boy!' Romoke smiled.

Funso got up. 'I'm not going to play again, mama,' he said; 'I want to stay with our visitor – I like her.'

'Come on, Funso, you see we are discussing here and it's not proper for children to stay where their parents are entertaining a visitor – OK?' Mama Agba reproved him. 'Now, Funso, go and play with your friends –we are discussing here!' she ordered.

Funso reluctantly walked out with his back.

'Oh, the boy is good and friendly,' remarked Romoke.

'That's Funso for you! He has a tender heart,' replied Mama Agba. She paused a bit. 'Now, you were about telling me about your situation, Romoke,' she said.

Romoke's mood went sad again as she remembered her predicament and imminent death. 'My story goes like this,' she began:'I used to be a committed Christian in my teens but I was lured by a friend into promiscuity….'

She narrated her story from how she got her baby and then threw him away to how she was impregnated by a guy on campus and had her womb damaged and then removed.

'The mother of all these misfortunes', she continued, 'is this: when I got to that guy's house – the guy who impregnated me, I discovered he had run away; and this moved me to… to buy –'

She burst into tears.

'Go on, my dear; go on,' Mama Agba encouraged her.

'Mama, I can't say it!' sobbed Romoke.

'Now listen, my daughter,' started Mama Agba, 'I want you to get this right, that there is still hope for you. God can still forgive you of your wrongs!'

Romoke gave her a contemptuous look.

'My dear,' she continued, 'I felt an inspiration – a message dropped in my spirit while you were telling your story.'

Romoke was not moved. She was at the brink of death; so then, of what use (she thought) could the message be to her?

'The message is this,' Mama Agba went on: 'You will not only be a mother again, you will also be a grandmother. This is what I sense the Holy Spirit asking me to tell you,

Romoke.'

Romoke burst into tears. 'Mama, please don't deceive me! I may dare to believe Jesus can still forgive me my sins, that I can still make it to Heaven; but please save me the agony of hearing those words you call message from God – save me from hearing them again! Although you're the second person to say this word of prophecy to me, and thus emphasizing it; yet I have now proved that it is false!'

Mama Agba leaned forward and scrutinized Romoke's eyes, surprised at her response.

'Mama, I poisoned myself in that bush a few minutes before you came to me, and I'll die anytime from now!' she sobbed. 'Ah, I wished I never took it! I wished I never took it!' she cried.

Mama Agba laid her hands on her head as her brow began to be covered with sweat.

'But I believe I heard from God,' she mused, her eyes filled with tears.

Romoke took out the polythene bag to show her the empty poison container. 'Look at the poison jar; I took the poison less than three minutes before you came to me!' she sobbed.

As she brought out the poison jar from inside the polythene bag, the piece of paper inside the polythene bag flew out.

'What is that? I mean what's on that piece of paper?' asked Mama Agba.

'I found it there; and the money I used to get the poison too, returned there. It should be a note from the Pharmacist I bought the poison from. I guessed he wanted to persuade me not to take the poison; so I intentionally avoided reading it then – I was resolute to die then,' Romoke replied and then burst into tears again.

Then she looked up as though to heaven.

'God,' she prayed, 'I know I am not fit to talk to You; but please hear me, if only this once! Jesus Christ, I don't want to die again. If at all possible, spare my life, Jesus! Oh please spare my life – please!' And then she burst into more tears.

'Why not read the note the Pharmacist put with the poison?' Mama Agba suggested.

'Of what use is it anymore, mama? It's too late!' replied a despaired Romoke.

'Take it and read it, my dear!' Mama Agba said emphatically.

'Okay, mama,' Romoke replied and she took up the note. She opened it and calmed herself down, and then she slowly read the content out.

What could be the content of the letter? Could it be a persuasion for Romoke to forebear taking the poison? But she had taken it already. Could it be words of encouragement to her so that she might be heartened by the words? If so, then it's of no use anymore. Could it be that the Pharmacist was sorry for his act of selling poison to someone who wanted to commit suicide – a crime that is as heinous as the attempt of suicide itself? Whatever the content was, it was what would soon move Romoke to more tears! And the note went thus:

Dear Young Lady,

As a Yoruba adage goes: 'Beheading is not the cure for a headache', I will not like you to take ending your life as the solution to life's difficulties– in whatever form they might have come to you – which are part of life. You're too young and too beautiful to be thinking of ending your life – in fact, a person shouldn't at all!

It is in the light of this that I decided, having been sure that you don't recognize how the stuff looks like, to 'sell' you a placebo instead of the stuff, and return the money to you.

Please, do not come to me to say anything about this, or even to thank me. I am doing this for God's sake. Stay alive!

Yours sincerely,
The Pharmacist.

Romoke was so stunned that she fell down, just rolling and rolling on the floor as tears of unutterable joy ran down from her eyes. She could not comprehend such mercy of God to her. Only what could come out of those dumbfounded lips of hers were: 'O my God! My God! My God!'

Oh, what explanation can be given this? Indeed, God's mercy impedes our nemesis! Oh, Romoke would not die! The best thing that had ever happened to her! Too wonderful for words!

She knelt down. Her tears now took another turn. This time around, they were the tears of repentance. She felt very unworthy of that goodness of God to her, that she could not but rededicate her life to the Jesus Christ who had been so faithful to seek her when she was too faithless to keep Him! She didn't know how best to show her gratitude to this wonderful, merciful Saviour more than for her to give Him the entirety of her life and being.

'Mama, please pray for me,' she said – 'I'm ready to live better for Jesus from now on!'

* * *

It was already evening that Sunday, about eight o'clock. Screams of the delighted children playing still filled the village air. The dust stains on their clothes looked like patches of gold in the gleaming moonlight. The children were so much enjoying their play that they seemed to be unmindful of time.

Mama Agba came out and stood in the entrance door of her house.

'Funso! Funso!' she called. Funso heard from afar.

'Ah, mama's looking for me – I'll be spanked tonight!' he exclaimed. 'Friends, I'm going home!' he said and then ran home as fast as he could. When he got beside the house and when Mama Agba had not yet seen him, he walked slowly and just replied(after about a minute and a half since Mama Agba had called him), 'Yes ma – I'm right here!'

Mama Agba, seeing him, laughed at his childish craftiness.

'Little children!' she chuckled. 'You weren't playing beside the house; tell me, you were far off, weren't you?' she said.

'Ye… Yes ma, I was,' replied Funso, rather abashed.

'Anyway, the dinner is ready; come inside,' said Mama Agba –'but don't play outside till it is dark again, OK?'

'OK ma,' replied Funso as he entered.

They sat at meal on the mat in the sitting room. Funso decided to sit beside their visitor Romoke. Mama Agba told Romoke that she would take her to her village, Ibupẹṣọ – for she had told her where her home was –and she told Funso to prepare his mind as they both would follow their visitor to Ibupẹṣọ village. Soon after the food, Funso slept off there on the mat in the sitting room, but Romoke and Mama Agba continued their discussion. Romoke still went on to tell Mama Agba her past; however, not with sorrow and despair this time around, but with joy that God had restored her hope.

'Mama, God so much loves me,' she said. 'This is the second time I would come to a point of total despair;but see how God intervened now, mama.'

'What was the first time, my daughter? Tell me,' said Mama Agba.

'I've told you before,' replied Romoke – 'it was the time I told you about, that I said I despaired when my father wanted to disown me because I didn't know who the father of my baby was, and so I went and threw away the baby somewhere.'

'Why could you have thrown away your baby for pity's sake?' said Mama Agba.

'Mama, I don't know what came over me then; as it came over me again this afternoon that I wanted to kill myself,' replied Romoke. 'I just woke up that morning and headed for a neighbouring village and abandoned the baby on one abandoned farmland; but when I felt so bad at it, I went back in order to carry my baby, only to discover that a wild animal had killed it,' she narrated.

'Ah! A wild animal killed it!' exclaimed a shocked Mama Agba. 'And what did your parents do?'

'My father disowned me! It took two years before he could pardon me completely – he took me back in 1978!'

'Wait a moment, it happened in 1976?' Mama Agba cut in.

'Yes, 1976 – late 1976.'

'Is it that the wild animal swallowed up the baby, not leaving a trace of it; or that it carried it away from there; or that it just killed it there?'

'We actually don't know, mama,' replied Romoke; 'but all that the wild animal left there was the swaddling clothes stained with the baby's blood.'

'Oh, my God, save me from this riddle!' exclaimed a puzzled Mama Agba.

'What happened, mama?' Romoke asked, rather puzzled.

'Where did you abandon the baby?' Mama Agba asked anxiously, not minding to answer Romoke's question.

'On one abandoned farmland.'

'I mean in which – okay, in which town was that abandoned farmland?'

'It's not in a town, mama; it's in a neighbouring village to my own village,' explained Romoke.

'A village – right. And what's the name of that village – I mean the one where you abandoned your baby?' enquired Mama Agba.

'It is Akatape village, mama.'

The old woman stood up amazed.

'Ah! See God! See God at work!' she exclaimed.

'What's it, mama?' asked a puzzled Romoke.

'Your baby – was it a boy or a girl?

'A boy, mama,' replied Romoke. 'But mama, what –?' She just froze.

A moment's absorbtion.

'*Abajọ*[59]!   Blood is thicker than water – no wonder he can't help liking her!' said the old woman.

'What, mama? Please tell me!' begged Romoke, who was more puzzled and had become more anxious.

Mama Agba looked at her and spoke in a gentle, low voice.

'God's ways are past finding out! My dear, the baby you abandoned on that deserted farmland in Akatape village, five years ago, is this five year old Funso, sleeping here! He belongs to you!'

'Huh!?'

She stared at Mama Agba and then at Funso in utter disbelief.

'Yes, my dear; this is the child you threw away!' the old woman said emphatically.

---

59 No wonder!

'Mama, how?' asked a bewildered Romoke.

Mama Agba sat down.

'Romoke, you see, I never knew you were the girl I saw that dawn on that deserted farmland'

'Huh? You saw me?'

Mama Agba smiled.

'Yes, my dear; I was in that same bush that early morning gathering firewood to cook for my youngest daughter who had then put to bed in Akatape....'

Mama Agba told the whole story of how she picked up the baby; and Romoke then knew that her baby was actually not devoured by a wild animal.

'...So I took him; and I named him "Funṣọ", from the words: "*Oluwafunmiṣọ*[60]" ,' concluded Mama Agba.

Romoke stood up, slowly, as a tear tricked down her face. She was dumbfounded. Her mind flashed back to when she was carrying the baby out of her room that day and heading for Akatape – '*I hope You'll forgive me, God. I hope You'll understand*'; flashed back to when she got to that deserted farmland – '*Where are You, God? Where?*' flashed back to when she bade the baby farewell, which she was abandoning there – '*...God watch over you while I can no more watch! Bye-bye!*' flashed back to when she returned there only to meet just blood-stained swaddling clothes –'*Ah! A wild animal has killed my baby!*' and flashed back to when she was left with no ray of hope – '*...now, there's nothing again! NOTHING AGAIN!!*'

And then she sank to her knees.

She couldn't just contain her emotions. She burst into tears. She just didn't know how to praise this God who had been gracious and merciful to her despite her unworthiness.

'Ah, my God, You've given me hope again! You've given

---

60 (Yoruba) Literally, 'God gives me to watch over'.

me hope again!'

* * *

Early on the day following, that is, on Monday, as they prepared to journey to Ibupẹsọ village, Mama Agba told Funso that he would henceforth be living with Romoke; that she was his mother. However, five year old Funso in the village was too little to understand what Mama Agba was saying. He had never thought on who his mother or his father was. All he knew was that he had Mama Agba whom he had grown up till that age to know, and who cared for him as a parent.

'Will you like to live with this lady, your mother?' Mama Agba asked, pointing at Romoke.

'My mother?' queried little Funso.'What is the meaning of "mother"?'

'The person that gave birth to you,' replied Romoke with a smile – 'I am your mother.'

'No, don't tell a lie,' said Funso –'Mama is my mother.'

'But do you want to live with the person you like?' asked Mama Agba.

'Who's that?' he asked.

'The visitor that came yesterday and you felt like staying with her,' replied Mama Agba.

'Hey! Where's she? Has she gone? I want to show her plenty of my toys!' said an eager Funso.

'She's the one in front of you!' replied Mama Agba.'Do you want to go with her?'

'Ha, yes!' Funso replied eagerly. 'Then she too will come to our house here to visit us too after I've gone to visit her!'

'You aren't going to visit, my dear; you're going to stay with me, and I'll really take care of you,' Romoke explained, trying to convince him.

'Stay! No, I'm not staying! It means I won't be seeing mama again? No, I'm not staying!' Funso demurred.

'Don't worry; I'll be coming to see you from time to time, Funso,' promised Mama Agba.

'My dear, I promise, I will take good care of you – you won't regret you come to stay with me,' said Romoke, squatting and holding his shoulders.

'OK, if I'd still be seeing mama and if my friend the visitor'

'No, say "my mama", not "my friend",' Mama Agba cut in.

'If my mama', continued Funso, 'would take care of me, I'll go with her.'

'Oh, thank you, my good son,' replied Romoke. She held him in warm embrace. 'Thank you, Funso. Thank you, my dear.'

Then they set out for Ibupẹsọ village very early that morning, boarding a bus going to Odo-Akan which they had waved down, standing at the main road.

Mama Agba was dressed in white *buba*[61] and *iro*[62], with white *gele*[63] of the same cloth. Funso looked particularly handsome in his *buba* and *ṣọọrọ*[64] of *Ankara* cloth. Funso was a handsome, fair-complexioned boy. He was rather tall for his age and was robust. His hair had a natural curl. His large nose stood attractively under his big, clear eyes.

Little Funnso sat on Romoke's lap in the bus. As the bus sped, Funso and Romoke were busy talking. Funso, who had never travelled before, asked a thousand and one questions, which ranged from reasonable ones to unreasonable and irrelevant ones. But Romoke answered all of them all the

61 A simple top.
62 Wrapper.
63 Headgear.
64 A simple pair of trousers.

same, as she enjoyed the mother-son chat. After quite a while of talking, little Funso slept off on Romoke's lap. Romoke could not describe the happiness she felt as her child whom she had long thought had been dead was now sleeping on her lap. She looked at his shut eyes. *Ah, I love him, and I'm really going to take care of him*!

And finally they arrived at Odo-Akan town and they decided, because of the long distance to Ibupẹṣọ village, to order a taxi cab to Ibupẹṣọ.

Inside the sitting room of Romoke's house, Segilola laid on a straw mat partly paralysed by stroke. Squatting beside her was Baba Oyeku, a native doctor renowned for helping people to elude death at critical times, who had resuscitated her some minutes after she had fainted the day before. Now, he had just made twenty-one short traditional therapeutic incisions on her: seven on the back of her head and seven each at the back of her left and right wrists. Omolara and Cynthia sat watching; and Rotimi was also there, preparing to leave for Itakuje village to search for Romoke everywhere he could search for her there. He would have gone the evening of the day before, but because of the critical state of Segilola's health he had delayed until that morning.

'Baba, but why has *Eleduwa*[65] decided to treat me this way?' Segilola asked Baba Oyeku.

'Daughter,' the old man replied, 'the dock, though naturally made to not be able to do without muddy streams, can only nod her head to the Creator in speechless complaints – we dare not question the ways and the sovereignty of the Supreme Being! However, my daughter, it is with patient and careful study that the "blind" bat with head downwards knows the path the birds take in the sky.'

'But Baba, will I never again be able to walk?'

'My daughter, however long it takes him, the stammerer

---

65 The Almighty

would eventually call "*Baba*[66]" . It is with constant trying that the parrot becomes versed in mimicking people's words; and it is with constant practice that the duck can fly a little bit like the flying birds: the lifeless limb today can by learning, limp tomorrow until it is no more limited in locomotion.'

Segilola began to lament.

'She who bares child, it is of child worries that she would die; and she who does not, it is equally of child worries that she would die. Romoke has chosen to cause me nothing but sorrow in old age. A child without a mother, our people say, will not dare to incur a wound on his or her back. Who do we have in this home, or who is "the tree behind her compound" that makes her that daring, being a fatherless child? Only God knows!'

She paused to swallow and then continued, looking up.

'*Baba Rọmọkẹ*[67] , please don't sleep in heaven over there; don't fold your arms in silence! Remember your family – your erring daughter and your poor wife, you left behind here!'

'Daughter,' Baba Oyeku put in, 'I shall be going to make plea on your behalf to Ẹla, the god of deliverance, and to make appeal to him with the sacrifice materials I demanded from you. What only remains on your part is for you to get the herbs, roots and barks I prescribed you and boil them for as long as the medicine in them can come out in its full spirit; and then you take them.'

'Ah, Baba, someone has already gone to fetch some herbs for her as early as dawn today before you came,' said Rotimi.

'Whose prescription did the person follow?' asked Baba Oyeku, rather angry.

'Baba, actually the person didn't follow anyone's prescription. She went on her own to fetch them,' replied

---

66 Father
67 O Romoke's Dad

Rotimi.

'Who's that?' asked Segilola.

'It is your brother-in-law's wife, mama,' replied Rotimi.

'Oh, Kikelomo!' said Segilola, discovering that it was her. 'But how would she cope with her health? So, she'd gone to the bush defying her present state just because of me – ah, that's very kind of her!'

Just then, Kikelomo entered from the backyard door and entered into the sitting room with a polythene bag full of various herbs, tree roots and tree barks. You could easily see her stomach protuberant which was bulging enough to push her long dress forward. Actually, our lady was then five months pregnant – pregnant again at last!

Kikelomo bowed to touch a knee to the ground, greeting Baba Oyeku. '*Ẹ k'aarọ, Baba* [68],' she said.

'*K'aarọ ọmọbinrin* ,[69]' Baba Oyeku replied. He turned to Rotimi. 'Is this the lady?'

'Yes, Baba,' replied Rotimi.

'Now daughter, who prescribed these herbs you've gone to fetch for this sick woman?'

'Actually, Baba, no one prescribed it; I decided to go and fetch it very early this morning,' replied Kikelomo.

'Don't you know that it is my job to prescribe them for her, and not your own duty?'

Kikelomo knelt down. 'I'm sorry, Baba. Actually, I did not know you would be coming this morning to treat her; I only meant to help mama. I'm sorry Baba.'

'All right, stand up. I'm amazed at your conduct, I must confess,' he remarked. 'Actually, frankly speaking, these therapeutic rituals and sacrifices that men demand from us don't wholly disentangle from the forces of illness as natural

---

68 Good morning, sir
69 Good morning, daughter

medicine with nothing attached,will do! Let me see the herbs you fetched.'

Kikelomo took them out and showed him. On checking everything, he was amazed. 'Oh, daughter, you got the exact ones I would have prescribed!'

'Baba, she's well versed in natural medicines, only that she wouldn't learn the ones of the traditional religion,' commented Segilola.

'Just natural medicine – good,'remarked Baba Oyeku. 'We cannot separate ourselves from nature's free gift – they are indispensable to us, as we also are to them.'

He then spoke softly, addressing Kikelomo. 'Daughter, we go sickly, we are deformed, we die, when the herbs, tree roots and tree barks to cure our ailments and ill health are just behind our houses. We die of malnutrition and we envy those in the cities, when healthful food is here with us in the village.'

He paused and then continued.

'As for the therapeutic rituals and traditional medicine, I sound this note to you:He dares not ventures into the traditional religion medicinethat bears no resolute heart and is disposed to sacrifice anything – and I mean anything – which the gods might demand; for the powers are not humans with a tender disposition: and who can stand in the time of repercussion? However, he is no fool who stays within the limits of nature's less demanding healing provisions to get health – that without a sacrifice. This I would say again to Kikelomo –the pasture is not as green as it appears from the other side of the fence!'

He paused.

'Children, I leave you in peace,' he said and then left.

'Mama, let me now be going – I pray I'd find her,' Rotimi said as he got up to leave for Itakuje village.

'All right; go well,' replied Segilola: '*ori oku orun yoo*

ṣ'ọna rẹ ni 're![70] ' she prayed.

The sound of a car parking was heard outside.

'Who could that be?' said Segilola. 'Go and check the car parking,' she said to Omolara who, with Cynthia, had been sitting quietly all along with them in the sitting room.

Rotimi stood there anxious, waiting to see who the visitor that would come in was. Omolara screamed with excitement on getting outside. Kikelomo and Cynthia immediately rushed out, and when they got there, they could not help but scream too. Rotimi stood by Segilola, to ensure that she kept calm.

'Ah, what's the scream about? What may be happening outside?' asked Segilola.

'Keep calm, mama; it sounds like shouts of excitement and not of chaos,' said Rotimi.

Outside Mama Agba didn't let Funnso come down from the cab at first – only Romoke and she came down. Kikelomo, Omolara and Cynthia took Romoke in with some sort of excitement. Then after they had all gone inside, Mama Agba let Funso come down from the cab, and she took him to the front of the house and made him wait there while she went inside, and the car zoomed off.

Romoke was shocked when she saw her mother lying down motionless on the mat in the sitting room.

'See what you've caused for me, Romoke – see it now! This is what my child will repay me with at old age – paralyses by stroke! This is how my child will say thank you for my struggles over her!' Segilola blurted.

Rotimi turned to Cynthia and Omolara. 'Oh, ladies, you can now go to your campus, as we won't want this matter to affect your studies. I think you understand. Now you've seen your friend in good state, uh? You may now take your leave.

---

70 May the fortune of the deceased grant you success in it!

We appreciate your visit. Thank you for coming.'

Omolara had known what that meant. She knew the man had cleverly spoken ironically. She realized they were least needed there and their presence there was an encumbrance. They stood up and after they had waved Romoke goodbye they left for their campus.

Romoke stood beside her mother speechless and with downcast eyes. She felt pity and sympathy for her poor mother who had laboured so much for her. *It would have been fairer if this has happened to me, and not to this poor woman! How happy I would have felt if it was me this happens to, instead of my poor mama! Ah she doesn't deserve this that I have caused her!* And a tear rolled down her face and dropped to the ground.

She went on her knees beside her mother. She wanted to beg but her lips quivered for fear, her eyes filled with tears.

'Romoke, it is high time you even killed me!' Segilola blurted out in the peak of sorrow and in despair. 'It is high time you hastened me to join your father!'

'Ah, please don't talk like this, *Ma'a mi*[71] ,'begged Romoke.

'Why shouldn't I, daughter? Why shouldn't I? What is the essence of old age if I will not eat the fruit of my labour, uh?'

'*Ma'a mi*, I know I have offended you so much that I don't deserve any blessing from you – I didn't keep to your counsel and warning; but please, pardon me! I have turned over a new leaf completely and permanently, *Ma'a mi*. I promise to make you happy from now on, and to take care of you. Please, pardon me, *Ma'a mi*,' begged Romoke, sniffing quietly.

'How do I know you have changed? How am I sure you

won't return to your past yet again? What's the possibility that this recurring issue won't happen the third time, uh?' queried Segilola.

'*Ma'a mi*, I have committed my life to God afresh and I've resolved to live better for Him from now on. Also, I'm willing to follow your instructions and pieces of advice to the letter now,' said Romoke.

'All right,' replied Segilola, 'I forgive you – you are my daughter, after all. Maybe I have been fated not to have a single joy over you; maybe my parenthood had been fated for tears in old age!'

'Mama, please don't despair; it's not like that,' Kikelomo said.

'What more is needed for parenting to be considered sour and full of hardship, than I have experienced over Romoke!?' retorted Segilola. 'Ah, I wish *Eleduwa* will comfort me in old age, but He choose not to! I grope for solace, but my hand is too numb to feel it and my eye too dim from many tears to see it! Let my ill-fated parenthood hasten my inevitable end and ease me of my struggles!' she cried out in the peak of sorrow.

She then looked at Mama Agba who had been sitting quietly all along. She greeted her and asked Romoke who she was. Romoke narrated the whole story about how she was rescued by Mama Agba; and they all expressed their gratitude to her. She then told them everything about her lost child, but now found, who they thought had been killed by some wild animal. And they were utterly astonished.

Mama Agba stood up gently and went out. Then she came in again, holding little Funso in her hand. 'And this is your daughter's child', she said, 'whom she threw away five years ago. *Mama Ṛọmọkẹ*[72] , here's your grandson – he's alive; he wasn't dead!'

---

72 Romoke's Mum

'Eh! *Kaṣa*[73]! , exclaimed Segilola. 'Ha, come here, my child!' she said, beckoning with her right hand which was not paralysed.

Funso went to her.

'Ha, sit down! Sit down beside me!'

He sat.

'Ha! *Ọba Adani-magbagbe*[74]! 'she exclaimed in wonder. 'So God hasn't yet forgotten us!'

Kikelomo and Rotimi looked on with utter astonishment. The former felt inexpressible joy, for she remembered when it all seemed that there was no more hope left for Romoke and yet she hoped against all hope, and had so rightly said to Romoke that day: '…And so, my girl, there is hope!'

'How I wish',said Segilola, 'I have the hands to carry you, my son!'

She gently placed his head against her bosom. 'Oh, God has remembered my tears! He has chosen to comfort me again! Romoke my daughter, it is now that I know that your Jesus has not forgotten you. It is now that I understand all that your auntie has been telling you from her Holy Book! And it is now that I believe – I wholly believe – that your Jesus is living, and that He can bring hope out of complete hopelessness! Come nearer, my daughter. Lay your head here too.'

Romoke placed her head on her bosom too. Segilola put her right hand over her daughter and her grandson's heads and gently pressed them against her bosom warmly, and tears welled up in her eyes and in Romoke's eyes too. Oh, the warmth and the emotion of the reunion between grandmother and grandson! Oh, the warmth of the embrace! Oh, how they produced in Segilola and Romoke precious and emotive memories!

---

73 Wow
74 The Creator-King who does not forget his creation.

'Romoke, will you please lead me in praying to this God who so much love us,' Segilola requested softly. 'I would have wished to sacrifice goat, or sheep, or maybe palm oil, and kolas too – just sacrifice them to Him, but I've already spent all I have on this illness; but then, there's one thing I have – just one: I will give Him my whole life – that is all I have to offer. Romoke, will you please pray for me.'

'Actually, that is the only thing Jesus Christ would have asked for – nothing more!' Romoke smiled. 'All right, let's pray, *Ma'a mi*. Could you say this prayer after me: Lord Jesus….'

* * *

Romoke afterwards decided not to return to her institution, as her mother's ill health would not make room for that. Because of her mother's state of health, she was constrained to stay at home with her –she was just left with no other option than to quit school. The rather demanding care of her found son too contributed to her decision to quit her university education.

Now, Romoke engaged in learning local weaving. Meanwhile, she had enrolled Funso in primary school, in Ibupẹsọ.

As years rolled by, Romoke soon became a skilled weaver. After her 'Freedom Ceremony' (a ceremony whereby an artisan in training is given the right by his or her trainer to own his or her own craft business and workshop), she worked on her own and soon became a veteran weaver. She was dutiful and diligent in her work to the point that she became renowned as one of the best local weavers in the entire region round about. Many people came to her all the way from surrounding villages and towns to patronise her weaving workshop, which was beside her father's house. Her fame spread all over, even to distant towns so much that some other weavers began to envy her.

Meanwhile, Kikelomo had had three children: the first a female, who was born in 1981, when her mother was thirty-five years old, was named Ayomide – a Yoruba name that means 'My joy has come'; the second, a male, who was born in 1982; and the third, also a male, who was born in 1983. It seemed Kikelomo and her husband Dekunle, on having an open door to reproduce, had seized it with both hands; in that immediately his wife's womb was opened, Dekunle rushed to bring three children out of it within the space of three years before he put a full stop!

Now, Funso really played the role of big brother to Ayomide, especially at the time when Ayomide was starting school (primary education),and Funso was just moving on toJ unior Secondary school– that was around 1987/88; for each began his or primary education(which was to take a period of six years) at about age six.

There was harmony and peace among these families of Bayetiri. Kikelomo's children –Ayomide and her two younger brothers, play often, especially in the evenings, in Romoke's father's house. Ayomide usually took her homework to Funso, who always put her through. In the evenings, when the moon glimmered in the dark sky, Funso, Ayomide and Ayomide's younger brothers would sit on stools around Segilola, who would sit in a deck chair in the front of the house. 'Tell us tales, grandma,' they would say. And grandma would begin, 'Alọ o[75]… 'And they would all respond, 'Alọ! [76]'

There was one quiet evening that Romoke was grinding pepper on the stone mill, stooping to grind it, and her mother was sitting by her; and they were discussing about how eminent people did patronize her weaving workshop. Some British men and women, had come to Odo-Akan town, and had visited the Ọba[77] of Odo-Akan to know and appreciate the culture of the people. Before they had returned, the Ọba

---

75 Story, story...
76 Story!
77 A Yoruba Traditional ruler.

had sent someone to lead them to Romoke's workshop; for the *Oba* had once lauded Romoke for dexterity in the weaving of traditional attires. When they got to her workshop and were amazed, and appreciated such a superb craftsmanship of traditional attires, they then bought many of them in a good sum of money and took them back overseas. And the day this actually happened was two days before this day that Romoke and her mother were discussing as she ground at the mill.

Romoke while grinding just became lost in thoughts and unconsciously stopped. Her mother looked at her intently for a while and then called, 'Romoke, Romoke! What's on your mind?'

Romoke was awoken from her deep thought. 'Ha, I didn't know when I stopped,' she said and then continued her work.

'Romoke, tell me; what is it you are thinking?' asked Segilola.

'*Ma'a mi*, it's something that I don't just understand. It's a question that's kept on bothering me since when I couldn't continue my university education anymore, and yet I've not found an answer to it.'

'A question?'

'Yes, *Ma'a mi.*'

'What's the question?'

'It's just that I've been confused. I don't just understand —'

'Understand what?'

'All right, may I ask, *Ma'a mi*: is it that I have been fated not to be a graduate in life? Do you know why I ask? You remember it was when I would have gained admission the first time in 1976, that the whole thing concerning losing my baby happened, and I lost that opportunity; and later on, my father died. When at last I had another opportunity to go to the university in 1979, I gained admission and I became a student, lo and behold, the same thing that happened to me in 1976 that hindered my first admission happened again, in another form! Now, I should have returned to school after the whole thing, but then, you now have a stroke, which makes it compulsory for me to quit my university education. *Ma'a mi*, have I been fated never to be a graduate? Or else, why did all these happen just to prevent or stop my university education? *Ma'a mi,* I don't understand, I must say!'

Segilola changed her sitting posture. Romoke left her grinding, took a stool and sat down.

Segilola cleared her throat.

'Romoke!' she called.

'Yes, *Ma'a mi?*' replied Romoke.

'Romoke!'

'Yes, *Ma'a mi?*'

'Romoke!'

'Yes? I'm listening, *Ma'a mi.*'

'How many times did I call you?'

'Three times, ma.'

'Now listen,' Segilola continued, 'there is only one thing you failed to realize from the outset that now led to your being unavoidably constrained to quit school. Let me teach you sound wisdom, my daughter; and "keep it in your left hand, lest being in your right hand you swallow it with the morsel". Now, whatever anyone loves so dearly and desires so desperately and he or she is disposed to do *just anything for,* even to the point of going beyond reasonable human limits or mortals' natural boundaries – my dear girl, Mother Nature has so much principled it that the person in question would not have that thing; and even if he or she gets it – with such a means – I'm afraid, it may be that very thing that will bring his or her misfortune!'

'Ah!' exclaimed Romoke.

'Yes, my daughter,' replied Segilola. 'Consider people who are desperate for money. The so much desperate ones that go ahead to make money rituals so as to become rich suddenly may eventually "*eat their pounded yam in yam form*[78]" , as the rituals may turn against them at the attempt, or attract terrible consequences in the evening of their granted prosperity! The armed robbers are another example of those that are desperate for money and get it but unfortunately die by it, or at least live a very uneasy life. Again, people that are too desperate for power or position may ever be denied it, somehow. That's how Mother Nature has principled it in life!'

'Ah, I've never heard this in this manner before!' exclaimed Romoke.

'My dear,' continued Segilola, 'the weakness you have from the outset is that you take your books as an idol, to the extent that you could do very abnormal things as throwing away your own baby because of it! That you love your "books"so much and take it seriously was not the problem, my dear – in fact, that is one pointer of making success in life with "books", I believe. Romoke, I must confess, I used to be impressed with your zeal towards "books". We didn't have such opportunities in our time; at least, only male children – and just a few of them, at that – were sent to school. So I was proud to see my daughter behave like those headmasters in the villages! But then, the problem came when your "books" became a god, my dear! Girls who you tell me don't mind sleeping with their"teachers"on your campus so that they can pass them, are also victims of this problem – they idolize "books", or maybe just grades!'

She paused and then continued.

'Do you know that, that you became a friend to what's-his-name – that you became a friend to that boy so he could put you through in your studies, had not made you go wrong

---

78 (A Yoruba idiomatic expression) That is to say, they would be disappointed or get into trouble.

at all –'

'Really?' queried a surprised Romoke.

'Yes, my dear – you didn't know his motives and intentions. Listen again, that you went to him and he taught you in his room also had not made you to go wrong –'

'Is that so?' she queried.

'Yes, daughter – you were only rather foolish. But, my dear girl, what should you be doing in his room, with no one else in the entire house except this young man alone – what should you be doing till a quarter past eight or so, in the evening, from around four thirty that evening? What? My girl, you showed sheer folly! That's where you got it wrong!'

'Ah! Now I see!' exclaimed Romoke.

'Listen, Romoke,' continued Segilola, 'when the Devil – or call it fate or whatever – noticed your weakness, he made use of it to bring about your downfall. You remember, it was in this area of your idolatry for your books –so much that you could do just anything for its sake– that you were caught in the web, so to speak, of that young man, and was raped – no, that wasn't rape – you were tempted, you were seduced and you succumbed! End of lesson! You can continue your grinding.'

Romoke breathed a sigh.

'Ah, thank you so much, *Ma'a mi!* I have learnt a lot. After I finish grinding, I'm going to really pray to God to turn my point of weakness into a point of strength!'

'And so will He do, my dear!'

Part Two

6

'I'll Love You Over And Over Again'

The black night was brightly illuminated by fireworks and made colourful by attractive Christmas lights. The high-street shops of Iga town – a big, fast developing town, located in south-western Nigeria – were flamboyantly decorated in Christmas decorations. There was an air of Yule. It was the Christmas Eve of 2007.

Off one of the town's high streets, a fenced elegant white bungalow stood. A bull dog barked fiercely behind the grand gate at the sight of the fireworks. From the sliding-glass window of a bedroom in the house, a man's shadow, pacing anxiously around, could be seen vaguely. The man was tall, fair-complexioned, hairy and handsome. He was clean-shaven with a neat moustache. He was well built and his build readily bespoke him a prosperous and fulfilled young man – and he was but thirty-one years old.

'What an awful Christmas eve this one is!' the man said as he peered through the window and looked outside. He then went back and lay on the bed. The wall clock struck twelve.

He switched on the main light and got up. 'It's twelve!' he said. 'I'd like to say Merry Christmas to someone, but who is there to give compliments to?'

He went to the dining table and switched on the light – his dinner which he prepared himself was still on the table. 'Where's appetite when a loved one lies sick in the hospital?' he muttered.'I wish the day should break right now and I'll go and see her right away!'

He turned off the light in the dining room, went back to the bedroom and lay down to sleep.

He had not slept up to five hours when he woke up. His mind wasn't at peace at all – a loved one was lying terribly sick in the hospital of an illness which the doctors had not yet succeeded in the correct diagnosis.

He tidied up and got dressed, and he managed to take a few slices of toast and a cup of tea. And then at about a quarter to seven in the morning, he set out in his car – a shiny black saloon – and headed for the hospital, The Federal Government Hospital, in that town Iga.

He drove rather slowly through the high streets, past the modern shopping mall which was by one side of the lane; past the elegant high-street banks; past the lofty offices at either side of the lane; past the Federal Polytechnic in that town. Then he soon drove into a traffic jam. And after about twenty minutes of being stuck in the traffic jam, the way was freer.

He was now speeding. And then his mind pondered slightly on a few things as he drove on.

'I cannot afford to lose her,' he mused; 'she's all I have – the only one I have, at least for now.'

He burst out singing in Pidgin English passionately, as he drove on:

Sweet mother, I no go forget you o

For da suffer wey you suffer for me o

Sweet mother o o o

Sweet mother e e e

[The words in Standard English go thus:

'Sweet mother, I will not forget you

For the hardships you went through for me

Oh sweet mother!

Oh sweet mother!'

With apologies to star artiste Nichos Mbaga's long-time Nigerian popular emotive music, especially popular in the 1970's.]

He sang and hummed,rocking from side to side behind the wheel as he drove.

Actually, his mother had played a crucial role in his success in life, especially in regards to his academics and carrier, so much that he could not afford to lose her, for she was then seriously sick of an illness that the doctors could not rightly diagnose. His mother had struggled through thick and thin to send him through the primary and secondary school. She had had to suspend her own university education – for she had been only a Senior School Certificate holder then – just for her son to be well educated. Luckily for both of them, the son had got a scholarship to study in the United Kingdom, courtesy of an oil company in Nigeria.

This man travelled to the United Kingdom to study Accounting while his mother, in the meantime, had the chance to get her BA degree in education in Nigeria through a correspondence course from overseas. While she was running her correspondence course, she also engaged in local craft as a means of livelihood.

When her son returned from the UK, he told his mother of his plan to further his studies in Accounting by sitting for the ICAN (Institute of Chartered Accountants of Nigeria) exams, which would qualify him to be a chartered accountant. His mother, who had further plans of gaining a master's degree in her own discipline by then, had to forgo them, at least for the meantime.

Now, the man had qualified as a chartered accountant and was really indebted to his mother, who was now at this time almost concluding her master's through correspondence course. This man, then, having become a fulfilled chartered accountant, having his own house and his own car, had decided to build a cute two-bedroom bungalow with en suite bathrooms in Iga for his mother and his old grandmother.

Now, he drove into a big street, and then to the gate of the magnificent hospital complex. At the entrance gate were the words boldly written: 'WELCOME TO THE FEDERAL GOVERNMENT HOSPITAL, IGA.' He drove in and parked. He came down from the car and entered into one the lofty blocks, carrying in his hand a basket with a food flask and fruits. He took the lift to the fourth floor and then headed for the ward where his mother was at the fourth floor.

He entered the ward and saw his mother. (By this time, it was about 8 o'clock in the morning.)He smiled and went to her. The mother was a woman of forty-nine. Her face were slightly wrinkled and her hair rather too grey for her age.

'Good morning, Mum,' the man said.

'Good morning, my good son,' the mother replied in a weak voice.

'I brought you a Christmas card, Mum, and I brought fired rice for you to celebrate the Christmas. Oh, I've even forgotten to say Merry Christmas – Merry Christmas, darling Mum.'He gave her the card.

'Same to you. Thank you. Oh, I remember – the doctor that's treating me since yesterday is a kind lady and she's been treating me with tender loving care; in fact, I've hardly seen such a caring doctor as that. This morning, she gave me a Christmas card'

She took it from under her pillow.

'See it –she just took special interest in me and she's just nice to me. Please, I'd like you to thank her for me. Her name is Doctor Olorunsanmi – Yemisi Olorunsanmi. I even got her mobile number and email address, and she's also got mine.'

'Mum, I see what you mean; but the doctor was only doing her own job, so it's quite needless to thank her specially,' the man explained.

'No, my son; this young lady went beyond the limits of duty to really take care of me. She just has a heart of gold. She'd come again and again to ask how I'm fairing; and I could read the concern and affection in her look each time she asked about my health. Please, help me thank her specially – she's in her office.'

'OK, I will if you insist.'

He brought out the bowl of fried rice with malt drink, which he had bought in a restaurant that morning.

'Will you now take your breakfast, Mum?' he said.

'Oh, thank you, my son. Your children will also take care of you! Thank you,' the mother said. 'What is it so special that I've done that makes you treat me so tenderly? I don't deserve this so much, I suppose.'

'Ha, Mum, you deserve it in every way,'he replied. 'You might have forgotten your labour over me, but I can't forget. I can't forget the hardship you went through for me. I love you, Mum –I'll love you over and over again!' he said.

'Thank you, my son.'

'My pleasure, ma.'

The man stood up and headed for the office of Dr. Yemisi Olorunsanmi – a young resident doctor in that hospital. His mother sat up to eat her meal. The man got to the door of the doctor's office and knocked.

'Yes, come in,' replied Dr. Yemisi.

He entered and, lo and behold, his eyes 'sparkled' at the sight of the ravishing lady, stunningly beautiful! She was a fair, tall and slender lady of twenty-five. She was cutely dressed in a soft green Western gown with lemon dots. Over her gown she wore a white hospital overall and hung a stethoscope across her neck. She had a dimple in both cheeks. She was raven-haired and soft-skinned, and her hair was a mass of curls. She wore a wristwatch with black leather straps and she wore a pair of tiny golden studs.

She gestured for the man to have his seat in front of her. He sat behind her desk, in front of her.

'How can I help you, please?'

'Actually, I'm here to thank you for your tender loving care for my mother who was admitted here yesterday –'

'What's your name, please?' Yemisi cut in.

'Oh, I'm sorry; I should have told you my name first of all,' he apologized. 'Funso is my name – Funso Bayetiri. I want to thank you for being so caring to my mother, Ms. Romoke Bayetiri. Thank you so much.'

'All right; you're most welcome,' replied Yemisi, smiling serenely.

Deep love for Yemisi was born in Funso Bayetiri. Even from the first moment he set his eyes on her he readily fell in love with her – it was love at first sight for him!

'We very much appreciate your kind gestures, Doctor... Doctor Ye...'

'Yemisi is the name, Yemisi Olorunsanmi.'

'Oh Doctor Olorunsanmi, I'm grateful for taking interest in my mother. She even said you gave her a Christmas card –'

Yemisi nodded.

'Oh we really appreciate it. Thank you.'

Funso gradually dropped his gaze to Yemisi's slender fingers on the desk and took note that no wedding ring adorned her ring finger.

There was an awkward pause, as they both looked down for a while. Funso slowly raised his gaze a little bit; and Yemisi too. Her eyes met his. Funso gave a slight smile. She chuckled and looked down immediately.

'You made me feel embarrassed,' she said.

'Oh, I'm sorry,' Funso said.

Oh, in any case, Funso had already passed across the message of admiration through his eyes!

'All right –let's go to your mother,' said Yemisi.

'All right – thank you,' replied Funso.

So, the woman that lay sick of the illness that hadn't been successfully diagnosed was actually Romoke Bayetiri, a forty-nine year old Romoke! Nobody that had known her in the late 1970's and the 1980's and then saw her at this particular time would readily recognize her; for she had changed so much in appearance. Her beauty was now fading. Her skin was becoming wrinkled. Her hair was fast turning grey and was receding, and her dark complexion seemed to have darkened even more. She looked older than her age. Perhaps, these were as a result of the misfortunes and the vicissitudes of life that she faced – or should we say, that faced her, earlier in life; and perhaps they were also as a result of her struggles over Funso and his education.

Romoke remained single mainly because she had lost her womb. She had only lived with her son Funso who had always taken care of her. Romoke, who had completed her first degree correspondence course on Mass Communication, was now running her master's degree also in the same discipline and through correspondence as well. Her plan was to become a lecturer after her master's, and then later on progress to run her Ph.D programme. 'The sky's the limit,' she always said – 'I'll never stop till I reach the top!'

***

It was the twilight of that day, the twenty-fifth of December, and Funso ambled along in his lawn alone. He was dressed casually in a red and blue polo shirt on blue jeans. He strolled with the easeful afterglow of that day's experience, his hand clasped together behind him.

His erstwhile worrisome thoughts had given way to a refreshing one, his erstwhile unquiet mood to an easeful one. Easement and a feeling of serenity had replaced worry and restlessness.

Funso's mind was filled with the thought of Yemisi Olorunsanmi. His heart was overwhelmed with love for her, and he could not help but think of her. The attraction had begun on his first sight of her and the feelings had been deepening since then. Even as he was ambling along in his lawn and she was not there, he could still see her clearly in his mind's eyes.

Funso went to bed that night rather elated.

* * *

As days rolled by, Yemisi closeness with Romoke increased. Yemisi took Romoke when the former saw the latter a virtuous woman – for Romoke had outgrown her former state of moral instability, as life experiences had made a sage woman of her – Yemisi took her as her own mother. She told Romoke most of her background, and that her mother was no more. She told her that her mother had actually died some minutes after she had given birth to her through a Caesarean section, the worry of it had once made her father stricken by stroke. She concluded by saying that since she had grown up to be a young woman, she had never known the solace of motherly care except in Romoke's arms of love.

Actually, this intimacy had begun with acquaintance on Christmas Eve when Romoke was admitted to the hospital in a serious condition. She had groaned in pain on the hospital bed as Dr. Yemisi Olorunsanmi with a senior colleague of hers attended to her.

Yemisi had not been her cheerful self that day.

'You look sad,Dr. Olorunsanmi,' her senior colleague had remarked – 'I hope there's nothing wrong?'

'Nothing sir,' she had replied.

'All right – I'll go and see the result of the test conducted on this patient– it should be out by now. You stay with her; I'll be back in a moment,' the senior colleague had said to her and left.

'Why are you sad,dear?' Romoke asked,as she was looking at Yemisi who was not aware of Romoke's studying her till she spoke.

'Oh, not to worry – no problem; you just keep calm,' Yemisi replied, feigning a smile.

'My dear, tell me what's the matter,' Romoke insisted – 'I won't be happy if you are not,' she added softly.

'Oh never mind my mood, mama; you just take your rest,' Yemisi said, putting her hand in hers.

Yemisi had developed a keen interest in Romoke since then, and the following day –the Christmas Day –she had offered her a Christmas card.

Yemisi then asked the older woman, after giving her the card – she asked: 'Is it ever possible, mama, for a lady, whose fiancé, pretending to truly love her and have won her heart, later on jilted her and goes ahead to court her friend – is it possible for the lady not to be hurt?'

Romoke breathed a sigh and then told her own story of the feigned interest of 'a certain man' in her – a man who had pretended to be purely interested in helping her with her academics, but had got a wrong intention to seduce her, which he succeeded doing. Romoke concluded: 'It is not what others do to us that hurts us – it is our own reaction. But then again, it is normal to be hurting, my dear; but even so, it is necessary to forgive!'

'I'm that jilted lady,' Yemisi said. 'And this is the second time I'm jilted; and the last guy now goes ahead to court my close friend –my close friend, mama!'

She burst into tears and Romoke patted her and gave her a tissue to pat her face dry. 'You have to forgive all the same, my dear,' she said softly – 'that's when you'll be happier, uh?'

'You're right, mama,' Yemisi said and then paused a bit, sobbing softly. Then at once she spoke. 'Look, those guys really hurt me, true; but I forgive them… I forgive them –at least,for God's sake!' And then she burst into tears again and Romoke patted her.

And since that time on, Yemisi, who had then been solaced and heartened by the sage older woman's words, had taken her as a mother figure. Now, as Yemisi became closer to Romoke she just couldn't help but like and be attracted to Funso.

***

It was Monday evening, the seventh of January, 2008. Schools and institutions, and private and government establishments, had resumed work, although the day's work in different establishments in Iga had either come or was coming to a close.

Funso, dressed in sky-blue long-sleeved shirt and a black suit with a black tie, and had a pair of shiny black loafers on – he was driving from his place of work, a chartered bank (in that Iga town), and was heading for The Federal Government Hospital. He was stuck in some traffic jams at a few points on his way, but at last, after about one and a half hours drive, he got to the Hospital. He came down from the car, carrying a basket of food flasks with him and went to Romoke's ward, in the fourth floor.

'Sorry Mum, I got stuck in traffic jams at some points on my way– I should have brought your food earlier than this time but I've brought your dinner along with it too,' he explained.

'Thank you, my son,' Romoke said – 'you will have children to take care of you,' she prayed.

'Amen,'he replied.

'Romoke began to eat and Funso waited. When she finished eating, he said, 'Mum, what about your friend? Has she come to check you today?'

'Oh, the young doctor!' Romoke said. 'I learnt she's not on call today.'

Funso paused for quite a while.

'Mum, how close has she been to you, or you to her?' he enquired.

'I can say to a good extent,' replied Romoke.

'You've been closer to her than I am – what do you know about her personality?'

'Why do you ask?'

'Why not answer my question first, Mum?'

'Okay – I've known her to be kind and tenderly caring; besides, she is mild-mannered and forgiving – but why the question?'

'Mum, do you also know whether she is engaged or not?'

Romoke's manner changed.

'Funso, I'd like you to forget about that and don't ask me things about that one!'

'Why, Mum? I must confess, I love her – I deeply love her, I must say!'

'Ha, Funso, for Heaven's sake, don't take it that way! She's been so friendly to me; I don't want you to bring the matter of the possibility of you marrying her into it, please!'

'But Mum, you know I won't lie to you, don't you?'

She nodded.

'Mum, I say I fell in love with her; I can't just help but love her! I'm sure she "is" my wife.'

'And do you want to approach her and propose to her?'

'Yes Mum.'

'Ah don't, Funso.'

'Why not?'

'At least, not around this time!'

'Then when should it be?'

'Probably next year 2009, or even –'

'Next year?'

'Or even not at all, Funso – forget the issue!'

'Why, Mum? Come on, tell me why!'

Romoke breathed a deep sigh of confusion. Funso looked straight at her. There was a brief pause. And then Romoke placed her hand into Funso's and spoke in a weak and low voice. 'I don't just want you to. It would be embarrassing, I suppose; don't you think so? She'd taken me for a mother figure, not for a future mother-in-law!'

'Is that it? Just that?' he said. He chuckled a bit. Then he held Romoke's hand firmly, warmly. 'Look, Mum, I see what you mean,' he said; 'but do you know that many waters cannot quench love? Love is as strong as death! My dear Mum, I love Yemisi – I deeply love her!'

***

Yemisi at that time was at the garden of her house in the

living quarters of the hospital – for she lived in the hospital staff quarters, and she was sitting under a tree, relaxing and enjoying the cool breeze. She was dressed in a white short-sleeved blouse on a white Caribbean skirt,and she had a pair of slippers on. She was seraphic and serenely beautiful in her casuals of white on white; and she looked like a beauty queen or a sweet angel.

As she pondered, her mind was fixed on Funso. She wondered why she couldn't help but like him. She began to develop an interest in him in a way she couldn't really explain. The thought of him were so easeful that it refreshed her like early morning dew on the green grass.

***

After Romoke had finally given him the go-ahead, Funso left the hospital and drove to the hospital quarters to see Yemisi.

He got to her flat and parked his car in front of it, and then went to the door and knocked. Yemisi, who had already come into the house from the garden, opened the door and was startled to see Funso, about whom she had just thought.

'What's up?' he said, giving her his hand.

'I'm cool – come inside,' she smiled, placing her hand in his. 'How's your day been?' she said, welcoming him in.

'Oh great, but not without its usual strain that accompanies our work in the bank,' he replied as he sat down in an armchair.

'What do I offer you? Do you care for malt drink, or what?' said Yemisi.

'No thanks. I'll prefer a cup of chilled water,' smiled Funso.

Yemisi served him a bottle of chilled water and went to her seat.Funso did not waste time beating about the bush,on his proposal; he simply went straight to the point that had brought him that evening. He took a little of the glass of water and put it down and then adjusted his posture, now facing her.

'Yemisi,' he began, 'actually, since the first day I set my eyes on you, I fell in love with you and the love has been deepening ever since day in, day out, as I become closer to you and know you more closely. And I feel God wants us to come together; wants us to build a home together.' He paused a bit and then spoke more softly. 'Yemisi, I love you and want to marry you.'

There was silence as Yemisi stood up slowly, and, thinking, walked slowly up and down at about the same point. Funso took a little more of the glass of water and put it down again.

Yemisi stopped abruptly and looked straight at him. He was now looking at her. 'No, sir! Forget it. I'm not interested!' she said emphatically.

Funso hung his head disappointed. Then he stood up gently and went to her. 'You should at least take time to consider it, and pray about it, before you conclude, Yemisi. This no is too instant and I believe is without thorough consideration. Please have a second thought, Yemisi – I love you.'

'A second thought isn't necessary, my brother,' replied Yemisi; 'forget about the issue and let's face other things – I've given you my answer!'

Funso breathed a sigh. He hesitated to go but Yemisi's look at that time was unwelcoming.

'All – All right, Yemisi. Have a nice night,' he said as he turned about slowly and headed towards the door.

'Thanks. Let me see you off,' Yemisi said.

She followed him to his car; and as Funso opened the door and was about entering the car, she said, 'Brother Funso!' Funso looked at her and gave a wan smile. 'I'm sorry for responding that way,' Yemisi said; 'I'll give it a second thought and pray about it!'

His expression changed. '*Are you giving me a reason to be hopeful?*'

'Don't worry; I promise to consider it and pray about it, and in some days time I'd let you know my reply,' she said.

'Thanks so much, Yemisi.'

'*You're welcome.*'

And as soon as he drove off, Yemisi texted Romoke, and the text was like this:

Mama, yr son came 2 propose 2 me just now. I suppose U have disclosed what I confided in U 2 him, and have motivated him 2 come 2 me.But why, mama?

- Yemisi

Romoke replied with a text messagethat went like:

My dear, I never told him anything about it or motivated him 2 propose 2 U, honestly. In fact, when he told me he wanted 2, I tried 2 discourage him but he was passionate. Pls believe me; he's absolutely unaware of our discussion.

Yemisi didn't reply back, which make Romoke rather worried.

***

It was around nine thirty that Monday night and Yemisi was talking with her father Mr. Olorunsanmi – a well-to-do cloth dealer, on her mobile phone. She told him of 'one Funso Bayetiri's proposal' to her and of her response. She had told him sometimes before of her former relationships and how the men had jilted her. Now she told him of the new proposal and how she responded to it.

She added that although she couldn't help being attracted to Funso, she wouldn't like to go into a relationship at the time,as she was afraid of being jilted again. Her father asked

\,

about how she got to know him and she told him everything.

'Now tell me Yemisi; do you love the man?' Mr. Olorunsanmi asked from the other end.

'Yes Dad, I love him; in fact I can't just help it.'

'That's it, my dear! That settles half of the matter!'

'How do you mean, Dad?'

'You see, Yemisi, marriage is all about love – if love is lacking in any of the partners towards the other, forget about it being able to last long.'

'So, Dad, what do I do now?'

'There's yet one question I want to ask you –'

'What's it?'

'Have you prayed about it?'

'Yes Dad; it was after I got up from my knees now that I called you.'

'And how was it?'

'Dad, I must confess, my feelings for him rather deepened. I felt like seeing him with me here like I'm missing him so much,' replied Yemisi.

'That's it! Correct!'Mr. Olorunsanmi exclaimed.

'What's it?'

'My daughter, would you like to marry him?'

'I would, but… but –'

'What's the but there, my dear? I know you're apprehensive, but there's nothing to worry about; a relationship anchored on love will stay!'

Yemisi was encouraged and it was as though her love was fuelled afresh, and her heart was aflame with the sacred fire of love.

'Dad, I'm ready to say yes to him; I'll love him through thick and thin!' she said confidently.

'Good! That's the spirit, my girl! Now, my dear, I suggest you still wait a little longer before answering him in the affirmative – test his perseverance some more.'

'I should still wait a little longer? But… but – anyway, if you say so. Thank you for advising me, Dad.'

'All right, my dear.'

'Good night!'

'Good night, dear. Sweet dreams.'

At that time while Yemisi was dropping the mobile phone at the end of her conversation with her father, Romoke in the Hospital, received a text message, coincidentally. She took up her mobile phone and read through the message – it was Funso that had sent it and he had sent it from his own house, although oblivious of the conversation between Yemisi and her father.

The text was like this:

I went 2 C her, this evning. Her response was NO @ 1st; L8R she said she'd think it over. I hope her response would B positive.

***

It had now been four weeks since Yemisi had told Funso that she would consider his proposal. She hadn't given Funso any answer – not a yes or a no.

Funso had just returned from work. He entered his room, took off his coat, loosened his tie, took off his shoes and sank on his bed exhausted. He didn't feel like eating, as he wasn't in a good mood.

'Why, for Heaven's sake?' he sighed.

He took his mobile phone and read Yemisi's last text inside him.

I promised you I'd take time to think over it. Don't worry; when I'm through I'll give you my answer.

He breathed a sigh and sat up.

'Why should she keep so long?' he said. 'This is the fourth week since I'd proposed to her. Each time I ask her about it, her reply has always been that when she's through she'd give me an answer.' His voice dropped to a growl. 'Does she mean God is too busy attending to countless people that she just has to wait there on a queue before getting His word!? Or does she need eternity to consider?'

Romoke in the hospital was also disturbed about the issue. Since the matter began, Yemisi had not said anything to her concerning it more than the fact that she was still considering the proposal. Romoke had feared that Yemisi had been offended that Funso had come to propose to her; suspecting that from the tone and the content of her message to her the day Funso had proposed.

Now Funso, sitting on his bed in his room, contemplated the thought of the possibility of a negative response. The possibility dawned on him like never before. He couldn't contemplate what it would be like to get a no for an answer. However, he resolved to persist even if her response would be a no, if perhaps it would turn to a yes; for he was somehow convinced that she was his helpmate.

He looked up, as though to Heaven, with a look that suggested a disturbed mind.

'Father,' he prayed, 'for how long will I wait? Hope deferred makes the heart sick –God, a discouraging response like Yemisi's response of "Wait", too, pours cold water on flaming love! I must confess, this deep love is challenged! I don't know why she's doing like this! Help me, God!'

* * *

That night, Yemisi, unable to sleep, was constrained to consider what needless worry she would have caused Funso by making him wait unduly for her response which she had already since the day he had proposed to her. She felt constrained to put herself in his shoes,and she knew Funso truly loved her. She remarked that her delayed response was rather unfair.

At least, I've proved his love genuine, for him not to have waivered till now. I feel so sorry – it's rather callous of me!

'Hm, I'll give him a call first thing in the morning. I'll give him my positive response.'

Her mobile phone rang. She rushed to pick it up.

I hope it's Funso.

She saw it was her father calling.

'Hello, Dad.'

'Hello, Yemisi. Sorry to disturb your sleep; I thought it urgent to speak with you –'

'Actually, I wasn't sleeping –'

'You're busy studying?'

'No I'm not – I hope there's no problem you call me now?'

'You see, Yemisi, I was woken by a terrifying dream just now –'

'A terrifying dream? How does it go?'

'I saw the young man Funso –'

'Huh! Ah, what…? OK, go on, Dad.'

'I saw Funso and in the dream I just knew he was the one – I saw him beckoning on you to come to him. You were willing and ready to go to him but I, standing by you, asked you to wait behind for quite a while; but by the time I released you to go to him, we discovered he had left!'

'Eh, my goodness!' Yemisi exclaimed, and then the phone conversation halted as there was then network service failure.

Yemisi tried calling her father again but the network intensity on her mobile was nil. She tried calling Funso also but the call wouldn't go through due to the network failure. She became so disturbed and quite apprehensive that Funso would drop the issue of marrying her, making the third person that would propose to her and later on break it up! She almost cried she had lost a rare chance, that she had lost Funso! She again tried dialling Funso's mobile number but it wouldn't go through. Before long she slept off, and she woke up around five thirty in the morning and found the network intensity on her mobile now full. 'Oh, thank God!' she breathed, grabbing her phone and dialling Funso as she also tried to get her nerves normalised.

Funso, in his house, was coming out of the bathroom when his mobile, which was on his bed, rang. He went to pick it up. He smiled when he saw it was Yemisi. He took the call as he sat on the bed.

'Hello, Yemisi. Good morning.'

'Hel – Hello, Brother Funso. How was your night?'

'Fine, thank you.'

'Erm, I just want to give you my response to your proposal.'

Funso adjusted his sitting posture, now sitting anxiously at the edge of the bed. 'Uh? You've finished considering it? What's the response? What's the –'

'Yes!' replied Yemisi, cutting in.

'I mean what's your response?'

'Yes!'

'Erm, I don't get – you mean your response is –'

'My response is "Yes" – I want to marry you!'

'Wow!' Funso burst out with delight as Yemisi dropped the conversation and Funso gazed blankly with his mobile a little bit away from his ear, for he was absolutely delighted.

He dialled Yemisi again.

'Yemisi,' he said, 'thank you so much. You've really refuelled my love, you know; and I promise I'll love you forever –I'll love you over and over again, my queen! Thank you, Yemisi.'

'Brother Funso,' Yemisi also began, 'actually, since our first meeting I have found myself taking a liking to you and I couldn't just help it. Now I'm pleased to be engaged to you. I love you, Brother Funso –'

'No Yemisi, call me "Funso" – omit the "brother",' said Funso.

'How easy do you think that'll be for me?' Yemisi said. 'You're a brother to me; you're my knight in shining armour and my marital head-to-be and –'

'Your sweetheart, your love,' Funso cut in – 'so simply call me by name.' He paused a bit. 'Yemisi, I love you,' he cooed.

'I love you too, Brother – oh, Funso – I love you, Funso.'

* * *

When Yemisi got to the hospital early that morning, it was reported to her that the patient Ms. Romoke Bayetiri had started to improve at a rather fast rate. She went to her ward to check up on it and for the first time did not meet her on the bed.

'Where's she?' Yemisi asked a nurse.

'She's gone to the bathroom to take her bath,' the nurse replied. 'If I'm correct, this is the first time she'd get up from her bed and walk by herself to the bathroom.'

'When did you notice this improvement?' asked Yemisi.

'This morning,madam,' the nurse replied. 'The nurses on the night duty said she actually got up from bed around five thirty this morning and told them she wanted to go and tidy up in the bathroom. When they wanted to help her, she asked them to allow her walk by herself. They said she was able to walk, holding the beds and the walls for support; while they followed her from behind. She's now taking her bath, while we go there from time to make sure she's all right.'

'You said she started regaining strength obviously at around five thirty this morning?'

'Yes, madam – five thirty this morning.'

Yemisi gazed up. She remembered that was about the time she gave Funso her response in the affirmative. Now, at this time, Romoke walked in from the bathroom, holding the beds and the wall for support.

'Ha, Doctor – good morning,' she said.

'Morning, mama,' replied Yemisi, bending her knees briskly. 'Gently as you walk mama!'

Romoke came to her bed and sat down.

'How's your health, mama?' asked Yemisi.

'Ah,I feel better now!' said Romoke. 'I'm now regaining strength gradually and the inflammation is rapidly healing.'

'What about the coughing?'

'That has stopped!' smiled Romoke. 'Since five thirty when I woke up this morning I've not coughed for once – it vanished before I woke up!'

'Oh, thank God!'

Now Romoke was improving daily in her health. When Funso told her about Yemisi's reply to his proposal to her, she was overjoyed. She felt as though the illness had completely gone. She loved Yemisi more and became closer to her. Her relation with her deepened as she now related with her not just as her doctor, or just as a friend,or just as a person she was a mother figure to, but now as her daughter-in-law-to-be!

* * *

Funso and Yemisi had now begun courtship. On Valentine's Day, Thursday 14th February, in the cool evening Funso and Yemisi, after that they had exchanged gifts and valentine cards and went to an eatery, went for a stroll on a seaside resort.

They gazed at the heave of the seas, as the seas leaped ecstatically, which rolled out and lapped around their feet, making a gentle sound, the waves also splashing onto the sandy beach. They beheld the turbulence in the midst of the waves that made a roar in the mighty waters. The sight of the waters was indeed splendid and the love stroll that evening was good fun for them both.

The sun had begun to drop gradually now and they were refreshed by the gloriously colourful sun set in the western sky. They sat down on the beach and chatted on.

'Sweetheart, you're a rare beauty of no match, for real!' Funso said, holding Yemisi's hand. 'As a matter of fact, you're the most beautiful and most angelic queen, with priceless endearing virtues, that I've ever met in all my thirty-one years plus on the Earth planet!'

She chuckled coyly.

'Look,' he continued, 'it's because I hadn't met you all those years that I remained single! I can't imagine sharing my heart through life with another person that is not you!'

She laughed.

'Of course – yeah, all those years as a single, I've simply been waiting for you! You see, Yemisi –'

Funso's mobile phone began to ring, interrupting him.

'Oh! What sort of interruption is this!' he said. 'Oh, it's mum!' He picked up the call. 'Hello, Mum.'

'Hello, Funso – how are you?'

'I'm good.'

'Now, Funso, I know it may not be very convenient

for you, but please, I'd appreciate it if you can come to the hospital here right away – I have a very urgent matter of some utmost importance, to discuss with you.'

'Urgent matter! What's it, Mum? Can't you say it on phone? I'm presently away from town with Yemisi.'

'Please, my good son, try and come now, so much as you can. I implore you – you will not know trouble – please come right away.'

'Aw! OK, I'll come when I'm through!'Funso replied and dropped the phone conversation and then smashed his fist on his thigh angrily. 'Oh Nonsense! What sort of interruption is this! I don't care – let's continue!'

'But what was it she said?' asked Yemisi.

'She said I should come to the hospital right away, that she has an urgent matter to discuss with me,' Funso replied.

'Is it that she has some problems concerning her health?' asked Yemisi.

'I don't think so,' replied Funso. 'If it's about her health she won't be calling me; she has nurses and your colleagues to attend to her. Let's forget about that for now and continue with our chat.'

'*Haba*[79] Funso, your mother wants to see you right now. Courtesy demands we put an end to our chat now and you go and see her at once – we don't know why she called you to come with such urgency; and besides, our parents should be obeyed.'

'See how she's broken our smoothly flowing chat! Oh, I hate things like this! I hate things like this!!' Funso shouted angrily.

'Don't worry, we'll still have more than enough moments for this,' said Yemisi – 'let's go.' She stood up.

'Allright,' replied Funso as he stood up also – 'I'll drop

---

79 Come on.

you at your house, and then from there I'll go and see her.'

'OK,' replied Yemisi, and they walked to his car.

* * *

Funso was sitting on a chair beside her mother, who was sitting on the hospital bed. He had come on her call as she wanted to tell him something very important.

Romoke wanted to open her mouth to speak, but she hesitated for fear. Her mind went back again to an incident, which the thought of it had come to her mind as fresh as wet foliage after heavy rain and as clear as the atmosphere after rain on a cool evening. When the thought had come at first before she dialled Funso, it left her in fright and in apprehension that she might die if she did not take some hard steps immediately. She had therefore called on Funso as part of the crucial steps.

Now, as she waited to be able to muster enough courage to speak, she became lost in a memory trance.

* * *

From the open window of a room on the top floor of a single-storey residential building in the town of Iga, an old woman looked into the street, which was full of traders and their customers all bustling along the way. Students were also beginning to return from their various schools, as the day's work had come to a close. The sun radiated above from the bright sky. Rays of the golden sun went through the open window into the room in the upstairs of the storey building. The apartment was a rented one.

'He'll soon be back; at least, students are now returning from school,' the woman said, turning inside, and addressing a younger woman sitting in the living room. The older woman was Segilola – a fifty-nine year old Segilola; and the younger, Romoke – a thirty-five year old Romoke. The year was 1993.

Segilola, who had got somewhat better regarding her health, went to Romoke walking with a pronounced limp, and sat down beside her.

'What has Funso gone to do in his former school? Hasn't he completed his secondary school some months ago?' asked Segilola.

'I also don't know specifically what he has gone for,' replied Romoke. 'He just told me the principal asked him to come, maybe for his school certificate result.'

Segilola sighed after which there was a brief pause.

'My daughter,' she said quietly, 'take good care of Funso your son. He is going to make your dreams come true as well as bring sweetness out of the very fountain that had brought you bitterness. Through him, the cat and the mouse will no more have a predatory relationship for the first time in their interaction.'

She paused a bit and then continued.

'Romoke, tell Funso the truth of his paternity details and everything about how you once abandoned him in the bush. I'm not pleased with how you've deprived him of the true knowledge of his paternity and his birth. I'm telling you, it's not right that you give him the impression that Mama Agba, now of blessed memory, who took him up from where you abandoned him, was his paternal grandma. You make the boy believe what is not true. Don't deprive the poor boy of the truth of everything, Romoke – including how you threw him away! I'm telling you, the earlier you tell him, the better! Particularly for you!'

'Mama, it's for the fear of hurting the poor boy's feeling that I kept it from him,' explained Romoke. 'And I fear what his reaction may be to the unpleasant story of my cruel attempt to get rid of him. Mama, I fear! Mmm, he even asked me of where his father was, yesterday again.'

'And what did you tell him?'

'I told him he has no father!'

'*Awu!*[80] How could you say he has no father? But what did he say to that?'

'He wondered how that was possible, when I wasn't Virgin Mary. He easily knew I was lying. But then, to support my point I explained to him that by the statement I meant his father is nowhere to be found.'

'And what did he say?'

'He was too curious to be satisfied with that answer. He asked what I meant by that. He said, "Was it that my father went out one day and did not return?' I said it wasn't. He said, "Was it that he travelled?" I said no. And when he said, "Is it that he is dead?" I replied in a riddle. I said: "It is difficult to know the condition of one of nine identical birds with you, but much more difficult or even impossible to know it when they are away from you in the forests" – and then he stopped asking questions, although he didn't likely understand my riddle. And I added: "What the eyes doesn't see, the heart doesn't grieve over". I'm sure he understands what the saying means.'

Segilola breathed a sigh.

'Daughter,' she said in a low voice and a serious tone, 'a child can only have as many clothes as an elder; he or she can't have as many rags. I am your mother; and no matter how you are of youthful wits, I still remain in a place to give you sage admonition. To be frank with you, you are doing the poor boy wrong by keeping the truth of the matter from him. You must tell him, as a matter of urgency, if you do not want his Maker and his fortune to fight you!'

'Actually, mama, I've already told him this morning that when he returns from his former school I'll tell him something, and it is this matter I intend to tell him – I mean the truth of the matter. I felt bad overnight at how I've been

---

80 Come on.

keeping him from knowing the truth of everything. But then, I've now decided to tell him everything as it is when he comes back.'

'You'd better do!' Segilola retorted, after which she paused a bit; and then she spoke more gravely. 'Listen carefully, Romoke, if you will keep Funso perpetually in delusions of his birth and paternity and of what you did to him shortly after his birth, I tell you my girl, you may only see the peripheral of your dreams coming true, but I doubt if you would see the giant of your hopes realised during your life! I pray that would not be for you!'

Scarcely had Segilola ended her words, when seventeen year old Funso dashed into the sitting room where Segilola and Romoke were. He oozed with a thrill of success and achievement. He had a big brown envelope in his hand which he gazed at continuously as he jumped up from one point to another, screaming for joy.

'*Ma'a mi* [81], I'm going to *Ilu Oyinbo*[82]!' he screamed as he dropped to a crouch beside Romoke. 'Look, *Ma'a mi*,' he said, bringing out two pieces of paper from the envelope.

Romoke stared at pieces of paper at first, and then she calmed her down to read the contents.

After going through the first, she burst out, 'Ha, Funso! You made all your papers in excellent grades! Five A3's, three A2's and one A1! Oh, that's my boy!'

'Huh?' exclaimed Segilola, who does not understand. 'What does that mean?'

He succeeded excellently, mama!' replied Romoke.

'*A dupẹ!* [83]' said Segilola.

'That's not all, *Ma'a mi*. Look!' Funso said, showing Romoke the other piece of paper – it was a printed letter.

---

81 Mum
82 White man's country
83 We thank God.

Romoke read the letter and was astonished at what she saw – Funso emerged the third best student in the West African Senior School Certificate Examination (WASSCE) in Nigeria that year; and not that only – an oil company in Nigeria in affiliation with a university in the United Kingdom was granting him (and with the first and the second best students in Nigeria in the WASSCE that year) a scholarship to the university in the UK to study whatever course they wanted to.

'You won a scholarship to the UK, Funso!!!' burst out an astonished Romoke, and she carried him up and put him down again, extremely excited. 'Ah, I'm proud of you, my boy! Wow! This is great! This is… oh, goodness me!'

'And I'm going by the start of next year – some months time!' added Funso.

'What is it? Tell me, my dear,' requested Segilola who did not understand what they were saying.

'Mama… mama, Funso just got a scholarship to study in a university in UK – he emerged the third best student in this year's school certificate exam nationwide!' explained Romoke.

'I don't understand,' said Segilola. 'What is s*uckho… suckhola… suckholasipu*, or what did you call it? I don't understand those words, *suckoo… suckoo certifi*.... Or what's the name? I don't get them. Explain to me – you know I didn't go to school like the two of you; so you don't expect me to get you with those *oyinbo*[84] words.'

'OK, let me explain better,' said Romoke. 'What's happening is that Funso sat for the Senior School Certificate Exam – what we call *idanwo oniwe-mẹwa* – and he came out the third best throughout the country'

'*Koda*[85]! ' exclaimed Segilola.

---

84 White man.
85 Wonderful.

'He', continued Romoke, 'is now given a scholarship – that is, his higher education would be sponsored – to study in the UK – what we call *Ilu Oyinbo*[86] –'

'*Kaṣa*[87]! ' exclaimed Segilola.

'And he would be going', concluded Romoke, 'in the new year, 1994.'

Segilola then started to chant Funnso's oriki. It is traditional in Yoruba land for families and individuals to have certain fixed encomiums, called in Yoruba "*oriki*."

As Segilola eulogized his grandson in Yoruba encomium, the latter knelt down beside the former in respect as his head 'swelled' because of high praises!

Romoke prepared pounded yam for her son, whom she had become very proud of. After eating, he rested on Romoke's lap in the bedroom, Romoke sitting on the bed with her back rested against the wall. Romoke placed her hand over him affectionately. Then she remembered when she had just got him back and travelling to Ibupẹṣọ from Itakuje in the bus, that Funso as a boy rested on her lap. And immediately she remembered that she had wanted to tell Funso the true account of his birth and everything she had done to him. Fear gripped her heart at once and tears gathered in her eyes.

Ah, I can't tell him now, not even at any time this period. I'll tell him some other time later – probably when he returns from his study abroad.

Funso, although oblivious of his mother's thinking, looked up into her eyes. '*Ma'a mi*, you said in the morning that you'd tell me something when I come back from the school. Why not tell me now?'

Romoke shook her head left and right briskly.

'It's no more necessary?' queried seventeen year-old Funso.

---

86 The White man's country.
87 Wow.

Romoke shook her head again, but more slowly, to mean, No it is not.

* * *

'You ain't speaking, Mum,' said thirty-two year-old Funso, sitting by her mother who was sitting on the hospital bed.

Romoke was awoken out of her deep contemplation, and a tear rolled down her face.

'What happened, Mum? You shed a tear. What, Mum?' asked a worried Funso.

Romoke looked straight ahead of her, staring at nothing in particular. She contemplated how she would tell him the true account of his birth and about his paternity which she had kept from him all this while, as she feared what this reaction might be, for he had loved her and taken it upon him to really care for her. Her facial expression went serious and determined.

'Funso,' she began, 'hmm – I don't know! – what I'm about to tell you may hurt your feelings; but even so,please pardon me. Hm, I've not told you all this while because I fear what your reaction would be – and I don't want to hurt your feelings; but I must tell you, I must tell you….'

By the time Romoke finished telling Funso everything, from about his paternity which was not known, to how she abandoned him on a deserted farmland in Akatape, to how she lost her womb, and to how she got Funso back –when she finished telling Funso everything, the latter flared up at the former in fury, for the first time in his life; and he left in anger, without Romoke being able to persuade him to forgive her. Romoke felt deeply sad. She knew she didn't deserve forgiveness from him. She felt sicker, sick for sorrow.

She called Yemisi.

'Hello, Yemisi.'

'Good evening, mama. How's your health?'

'It's improving bit by bit. Thank you. I just want to –'

'You might be wondering that you're not seeing me these days in the ward; it's due to my leave – I'm on a month's leave,' said Yemisi, interrupting.

'All right,' said Romoke – 'and you should take enough time to rest. Now, I just want to tell you to help me beg your fiancé –'

'What happened, mama?' Yemisi cut in.

'He's angry and bitter –'

'With who?'

'With me. Actually –'

'For what? Why is he angry with you?'

'Actually,' Romoke continued, 'it's worth it. It's the story I told you that day about my past – the story of me losing my womb, but especially how I once threw away my son and got him back –'

'I remember.'

'That baby I threw away and later got back when he was a boy, is Funso; and I just told him the whole story now and he was deeply hurt –he just left now in a fury,' explained Romoke.

'Aw, mama, you shouldn't have waited this long before telling him!' reproved Yemisi. 'No, you didn't do well as to that!'

'I admit, Yemisi. I admit,' said Romoke. 'It was for the fear of hurting his feelings,not knowing what his reaction could be, that I've been keeping it from him all this while; but I admit I was wrong not to have told him since and he's right to have reacted that way –I admit.'

'Don't worry, mama; I'll go to him right away. I'll talk to him; just keep your mind at rest,' said Yemisi.

'Ah, thank you, my dear! Thank you,' replied Romoke.

'All right, mama.'

'Bye, my dear.'

'OK, bye, mama.'

* * *

Funso was sitting down on the porch of his elegant white bungalow, and his bull dog frolicked around him, wagging its tail, although he didn't respond to it. He sat with his elbow rested on his knees and his chin sunk in his palms. His heart had been deeply hurt. He couldn't bear the thought that this same mother of his, that he adored and cared so much for, and for whose sake he had denied his eyes of sound sleep on Christmas Eve– that this same mother of his had once abandoned him on one bushy farmland some thirty-two years earlier, probably with the wish that he should die there. And yet she had kept this from him all these thirty-two years! Ah,unbearable! Yes, so unbearable was the thought that it brought a tear trickling down the eye of a strong, grown-up man as Funso. Indeed, it was unbearable!

He wiped the tear. 'Let her rot and die on that sick bed!' he growled with bitterness.

What if a wild animal had maimed me, that day?

'*Kai!* Too awful too imagine!' he grunted with a grimace.

He stood up and paced about angrily.

'She hasn't seen anything yet; she'll die bit by bit! She's not my mum, never! She'd disowned me when I was a baby; now the table is turned, the table is turned, I'll revenge! I'll leave her too now, now when she's at death's cold grip! I will revenge on her!'

At that time, Yemisi's car, a cream hatchback, whizzed to Funso's gate and halted. Funso ordered the gatekeeper to open the gate when he saw that it was her. He opened it and

Yemisi drove in and parked. She came down from the car and went to Funso.

'Sweetheart, I know how you feel,' she said with a soft, gentle voice. 'Let's go inside.'

They went inside and sat in the living room on a two-seater sofa and talked. Yemisi spoke softly, encouraging him to forgive his mother, stating that God also forgives us when we sin, after all.

'Yemisi, it's not possible!' Funso demurred. 'Do you know the gravity of what she did? Don't you realise how long enough she'd kept me from knowing the truth of the matter? Or, wait a moment, what if a wild animal had killed me or maimed me on that bush where she dumped me, uh? What if I had died before my eight day – will you see me today to console like this, Yemisi? Will you be engaged to me as you are today, uh?'

'But sweetheart, God preserved your life! God preserved your life!' Yemisi said. 'Could you at all have kept yourself, there, from being killed or maimed by wild animals or from being carried away by ritual killers? Were you the one who protected yourself from them? Darling, it was God and God alone!'

Funso breathed a sigh. 'But I cannot forgive her. I hate her with passion!'

'Ah, Funso!' Yemisi exclaimed. 'Please, don't allow bitterness to spring up in you. You must love your mother regardless of all these; you must love her! She needs you the most at this time. Worry at this age won't help her.'

'I don't care!' Funso shouted with a shrug. 'To hell with her! To hell with her!' he flared.

She moved closer to him and spoke more quietly.

'Funso, God forbid, but if it happens that I make some kind of bad mistake too, it certainly means you'd not love me again; it means you'll turn to hate me.'

Funso felt rather awkward. He crouched down beside her, placing one hand in hers and the other on her shoulder.

'Sweetheart, I'm sorry – I love you and will continue to love you come rain, come shine. As a matter of fact, even if you do something bad and everybody in the world scolds you, Yemisi, I will still accept you and in privacy correct you, even still with love. I can't cease to love you. My sweetheart, I'll love you over and over again!' And he kissed her hand gallantly.

'But won't you forgive your mother and love her again?' Yemisi queried as he got up to his seat.

He paused a bit and then sighed.

'Hmm, it's not as easy as you think, Yemisi!' he said in a weak, low voice.

Yemisi breathed a sigh.

'I think I understand how you feel. I'm sorry if I don't seem to understand all. I'm sorry. I also have twice been hurt very much, but perhaps not as much as you are now. I was jilted twice, and I never expected that from those guys. The most painful thing was that my last fiancé after he jilted me then got engaged to a close friend. But then, I got the grace to forgive and I forgave those two guys, all the same; although it seemed impossible at first.'

'Let's not deceive ourselves – this thing is not easy!' Funso said.

'Yes, to be candid, it's not easy –but mind you, it is not impossible!' Yemisi remarked.

Funso let out a sigh.

'What you need', Yemisi continued, 'is God's grace to forgive. But you just have to forgive Mama – after all, we all commit serious sins against God and yet He pardons us. I'll be praying for you.'

'Thank you, Yemisi,' Funso said.

Yemisi stood up to leave and Funso saw her off to her car. The gatekeeper opened the gate and she drove off. Funso returned inside. He didn't feel like eating as he was not in a good mood. He just managed to take little Corn Flakes and went to bed; but then, he just lay awake all through the night. His eyes knew no sleep, not even a doze, and the night seemed so long to him.

By the time he got up from bed at four thirty in the morning, he felt his head aching as though some carpenters were doing some roofing work on the 'roof' of his head. He seemed to hear every sound echo in his ears. He stood up, only to see everything around him turned like a merry-go-round;and his temperature had started to rise, too.

By the time he finished taking his bath, he had realized he wouldn't be able to go to work. Funso was in an exalted post and status in his working place. He was the second in the management hierarchy of the bank where he worked in Iga and it is the headquarters for the branches in the region. Nonetheless, he phoned his head to get a sick leave. And his leave was granted.

He hoped to rest that Friday but he just could not. His eyes craved for sleep but couldn't find it. When it was evening, he thought of taking some sleep tablets but later decided to call Yemisi who would be in the better place to prescribe him drugs.

When he called her and told her about his state of health and also telling her that he had taken a sick leave, she promised to come to him.

By the time Yemisi got to his house, Funso was already sleeping. It was the sound of the horn of her car and the boom of her car driving in that woke him up and he came out to receive her.

They entered and sat down. Yemisi asked of how he was feeling at the time. He had got much better but he wasn't perfectly all right, and he told her how he was feeling.

Yemisi only advised him to take time to have enough rest and didn't even prescribe him any 'special tablet' or any sleeping pill other than a few familiar tablets. She also gave him some medical tips to help keep him at ease. She promised to check on him the following morning, to know whether his health improved.

On Saturday morning, she checked on him as she had promised. After she entered and they sat together in the living room, Funso lodged another type of complaint concerning his health. He told Yemisi that he couldn't have a sound sleep through the night and that from time to time he felt being pressed to the bed by some 'unseen force'. At anytime the force pressed him, he would lose his voice and wouldn't be able to cry out. He would be somewhat transfixed on the bed, his mouth too heavy to open and his shut eyes difficult to open. And after a while, he would be released, as it were, and he would attempt sleeping again, only to be disturbed again by that strange thing before he would have gone deep in his sleep. And on and on that went till daybreak.

'What type of drug', he asked, concluding, 'will you prescribe me for this abnormality?'

Yemisi chuckled.'You see, sweetheart, medically this could be termed hallucination. Hallucinations could be a symptom of an illness or could be caused by drugs –and high temperatures too cause them. Now, we can treat the actual illness rather than the symptoms.'

She paused and then continued.

'Look, sweetheart, when a doctor can't arrive at an accurate diagnosis of an illness, their medical treatment of the patient is quite unlikely to cure the illness. Now, if what is discovered of the illness are the secondary causes rather than the actual cause and only the secondary causes are addressed, I'm telling you, the illness would seem cured but the root of it would still be living unharmed, so to speak.' She paused a bit and in a subdued voice and a matter-of-fact tone she said,

'Sweetheart, I have diagnosed your ailment and known the actual cause –'

'What's it? Tell me; what's it?'Funso asked eagerly.

'I'd like you', continued Yemisi,'to let me treat the actual cause rather than the secondary – if you want it, though.'

'*Haba*, why won't I want it?' said Funso. 'You tell me what and what to do, and I'll do them right away!' he said eagerly.

'All right,' said Yemisi. 'I have diagnosed your ailment to be as a result of a deeply "hurt" "heart", the "wound" "infected" with resentment and bitterness!'

Funso's expression of eagerness faded away instantly and he turned slightly away from her. She moved nearer him and spoke softly.

'You see how you lack peace of mind and rest, just because of this issue. I know it's not easy, but please, for God's sake, forgive your mother, uh?'

He stood up.

'My mother or what did you just say!?' he shouted angrily. 'She's no more my mother! I disown her! I dis–'

His mobile started to ring. He took it up from the two-seater sofa where it was lying, and then he threw it back on the sofa.

'Why did you drop it?' asked Yemisi.

'It's her,' replied Funso.

'Who? Your mother?'

He nodded.

The ringing stopped. After a short while, the phone started to ring again.

'Pick up the phone, Funso,' said Yemisi; 'don't hate your own mother!'

Funso did not respond. After a while, the ringing stopped.

He took the phone and switched it off.

He then paced about awhile and then went to the wall and leaned on it with a hand, and resting his face on the hand.

Yemisi stood up and went to him. She placed her hand on his shoulder and spoke softly.

'Funso, I know it's not an easy thing, but you just have to forgive her if you must receive mercy from God and if you must continue to have His blessings. We also wrong God! We also do things that sadden Him more than mama has done to you – but doesn't He forgive us when we ask for pardon? If He were to repay us according to our wrongdoings, not one person would be alive today! I know you're deeply hurt – there's nobody this will happen to and won't be hurting; but if we have to dwell on yesterday's matters that hurt us, we won't have a person to befriend– so our elders say.'

Funso turned around. Tears had gathered in his eyes.And he spoke in a low, deep, shaky voice.

'She's hurt me to the heart. She attempted killing me! If not for God – if not for God, I will not be still living; I'd have died before my eight day! Ah, she lied to me that the woman who carried me from where she dumped me, and who she said brought me up till I was five – she lied to me that she was actually my paternal grandma! Good heavens, she kept me in delusion these long years! Ah, I loved my mother, Heaven knows! I loved deeply this same woman who would have terminated my life when I was only a few days old! But only God did not allow her! Ah, no wonder! No wonder she always says she doesn't deserve the care I give her! Ah!'

He looked up.

'God, how do you expect me to forgive the woman who would have killed me, had she had her way!?' he blurted, his voice laden with hurt and bitterness.

Yemisi went straight on her two knees, and she begged him earnestly, a tear slowly rolling down her face.

'Sweetheart, I beg of you do not allow resentment and bitterness to mar your good relationship with God or to hinder our smooth-going relationship. Even if you will not forgive mama for my sake, I beg you please forgive her for Christ's own sake – *please*!'

Funso was moved and he took her up from her knees as a tear dropped from his own eyes. He put his two hands in hers and looked into her eyes as he spoke with a low, trembling voice.

'Yes, sweetheart, my mum deeply hurt me–but don't I hurt God even more? I hurt God too, but He still accepts me with all my frailties! Sweetheart, I forgive my mum…I forgive her from my heart…from my heart!' And with that they embraced, hanging their necks on each other's shoulders, and sobbing.

* * *

In the evening of that Saturday, Funso appeared in Romoke's ward. Romoke was sitting on her bed with the Christmas card Funso had given her in her hand. She was reading through the words dejectedly.

When she raised her head, she saw him coming into the ward. Fear gripped her. They both looked at each other. Neither of them smiled. Neither of them frowned. Funso eventually stared her down till he came to her bedside and sat down. He still did not smile. He still did not frown. He took her hand and clasped it in his. She was terrified. And now he gave a gentle smile. Then he spoke – softly. 'Mum, I forgive you,' he said; I still love you.'

Romoke breathed a deep sigh of relief.

'Funso,' she said, 'please, don't be annoyed with me. I know I've really offended you. I know I hurt you. But please don't be annoyed with me, I beg you.'

'Mum, I've forgiven you, and I mean it. God has worked

on my heart and given me the grace to forgive. Now, I don't only forgive you, I also forget what you did!'

'Thank you, my son.'

'Look, I'll love you over and over again – and now I mean it more! Nothing on earth will make me cease to love you!'

'Thank you. Thank you,' Romoke said. She paused a bit. 'Funso, try to see the doctor before you go home –he asked you to see him,' she said.

'Who's that?'

'Doctor Kingsley – the consultant in charge of my treatment.'

'What's the matter? Is something wrong?'

'He didn't tell me what he wants to see you for. He only said when you come he'd like to see you and he'd also come and see me.'

'OK, where's he?'

'His office is the fourth door after Yemisi's office. You'd see the tag with "DR. H. Z. KINGSLEY" on the door.'

'OK, let me go now.'

He went there and saw the doctor. Dr. Kingsley told him that Romoke was then strong and would be discharged, and that she would have to be coming for medical check-up for some time. He said that it was since morning that he would have discharged her; but that when he was told, on asking, that Funso (who was responsible for the care of the woman) wouldn't come to the hospital for quite a while, he had delayed to tell Romoke that she had been fit for discharge. But now he was discharging her!

Funso paid all the hospital bills and then took her into his car and drove her to her house. Old Segilola at home was happy to see Romoke again, for she had been disturbed and apprehensive all along. Now they had cause to jubilate as though their own New Year festivity was just beginning. Romoke gave a million thanks to her son who had so much taken care of her. A thing of joy it was for them that Romoke did not die of that strange illness.

'Oh let me call Yemisi and tell her I've been discharged,' said Romoke, taking up her mobile phone. She dialled Yemisi's mobile number.

Yemisi took up the call.

'Hello mama,' Yemisi said at the other end.

'Hello, my good daughter,' beamed Romoke.

'How's your health, mama?'

'Oh, I'm very fine! I was just about telling you I've been discharged – just this evening!'

'Oh good! I'm happy to hear that!'

'Thank you, my dear,' said Romoke. 'In fact, I really appreciate your treating me lovingly. But for these, I won't be as strong as I am now– thanks so much, Yemisi.'

'Oh, not at all. It's a pleasure, mama.'

'Also, Funso and I are going to come at some time to formally say thank you.'

'*Haba*, mama, you needn't bother yourself with that; it's just not necessary.'

'No, Yemisi, you deserve it and I won't want to take you for granted.'

'It's all right.'

'When would it be convenient for you?' enquired Romoke. 'Will Saturday be okay?'

'Oh yes, I'll be home Saturday – it's okay,' replied Yemisi.

Romoke took the mobile away from her ear, turning to Funso. 'Is Saturday evening okay for us to pay her a visit?'

'Erm, I think I should be OK,' replied Funso.

Romoke resumed the conversation.

'OK, we're coming Saturday – Saturday evening. How about that?'

'It's all right. I'll be expecting you.'

'Thank you, my dear. Goodbye.'

'Bye!'

Romoke breathed a sigh of delight and then paused. 'There's something that keeps on bothering me and that I'd like to ask her come next week Saturday,' she said.

'What's it? Do you mind sharing it?' asked Funso.

'I don't mind,' replied Romoke and then paused a bit. 'Hmm, it is this….'

7

'You Again?'

It was a Saturday evening, a week after Romoke was discharged from the hospital and also the day that Romoke and Funso's thank you visit to Yemisi had been slated for.

We could see Yemisi sitting in an armchair with a glass of fruit juice beside her on a stool, and on her lap was a laptop on which she was surfing the Internet. She was actually chatting with her father. The door bell rang.

'Who's that? Come in, the door's not locked,' she said.

Funso and his mother entered.

'Oh, you're welcome, mama. Welcome, sweetheart,' she said. 'Have your seat please.'

'I suppose you're somewhat occupied,' said Romoke. 'I hope we won't –'

'*Haba*, not at all mama,' Yemisi put in. 'I'm just chatting with dad and he even said he's coming to Iga here the Sunday of the week after next, and he'll be pleased to see you. Come, why not chat with him mama?'

'OK, my dear,' said Romoke.

Yemisi informed her father through the chat that Funso and his mother were then around and that Romoke would like to have a chat with him.

Romoke took over and the brief chat between Ms. Bayetiri and Mr. Olorunsanmi.

'Hello sir,' Romoke typed in.

'Hello madam, pleased to meet you.'

'The pleasure is actually mine sir.'

'Yemisi told me how you've been a mother figure to her – thanks so much madam.'

'No, I should thank you for raising her up to be such a precious gift to us! Thank you sir.'

'Oh, don't mention it.'

'We promise we'll take good care of our wife!'

'Thanks for that, madam. Now I'll be coming to Iga the week after the next – precisely on Sunday then, for a particular programme, after which I'll check on you.'

'We'll be expecting.'

'And mind you,' added Mr. Olorunsanmi, 'that's not the formal introduction!'

'I know,' replied Romoke; 'we're still coming for the formal introduction – in a rather grand style!'

'When your son must have to fall prostrate for his in-laws-to-be!' Mr. Olorunsanmi joked.

'Ha! Ha!' Romoke typed . '*Abi o!*[88] '

'God spare us till then,' prayed Mr. Olorunsanmi.

'Amen – Should I call Yemisi to take over?'

'All right.'

---

88 Oh really!

She called Yemisi over.

'So Dad, we'll be expecting you,' Yemisi typed.

'OK Yemisi,' replied Mr. Olorunsanmi. 'Let me release you to attend to your people. Take care, dear.'

'Thanks, Dad. Luv you!'

'I love you too, my dear. Bye.'

'Bye!'

Yemisi logged out on the Internet and shut down her laptop. Then she breathed a sigh of delight and turned to them. 'You're welcome once again!' she smiled.

She went to Funso and held his hand.

'How are you today, darling?' she said.

'I'm cool, thank you,' replied Funso. 'You're looking particularly lovely this evening,' he remarked with a smile.

She chuckled.

'Thank you. Thanks so much,' she said.

She brought and served them chilled fruit juice with packets of digestives.

'Yemisi,' Romoke said, 'I really appreciate your tender loving care for me when I was admitted – thank you so much. I'm very greatful.'

'You're welcome, mama,' she replied softly.

'Not only that, I'm also very grateful to you for consenting to Funso's proposal to –'

Funso cut her short. 'Mum, I'm the one marrying her, not you. So let me do the thanking her myself, uh? Don't help me – thanks!' he said jokingly.

'I'm sorry sir for not minding my own business!' Romoke joked.

Funso then cleared his throat loudly, as though set for serious business. He went over to Yemisi who was sitting in an armchair, and crouched down beside her. He clasped her hand in his and looked into her eyes. She became terribly shy.

'Sweetheart, my angel, my queen!' Funso began. 'A million thanks won't do in expressing my thanks to you for giving your heart to me! Priceless princess, my rose, my heart, my love! Goodness, what angelic beauty I've found in a lady! I can't but wonder at the power of your beauty, of your smile, of your eyes! I can't but marvel at the magnetism of your love! O sweet damsel, my baby, me your knight could not but lose my heart to you! I've lost my heart to you!' And with that he gave her hand a gentle kiss.

Yemisi was extremely shy at his romantic praise, so shy that she felt as though the ground should just open under her feet and she should just sink in. She couldn't open her mouth to say a word. But then she couldn't help giving coy chuckles again and again.

'And is that not too much?' said Romoke, feeling awkward.

'It's not you I'm praising, Mum; after all, it's not you I wooed!' Funso replied.

'All right sir; I keep my mouth shut!' she said, holding her lips.

'Remove your hand from your lips – I'm done with praising my angel!' he said as he got up and went over to his seat.

Yemisi breathed a sigh and spoke at last.

'Ha, Funso! You almost made me intoxicated, overdosing me with that! And I'd have blushed scarlet from your overdose if I were White!'

He giggled.

'Oh, my doctor-patient, I'm so sorry; it's because I'm only a quack! Whoops, I let the cat out of the bag myself!' he joked.

They laughed, after which there was silence.

Romoke spoke.

'Mm, Yemisi dear.'

'Yes, mama?'

Yemisi changed her sitting posture.

'Yemisi, there's this question', Romoke went on,'that's been on my mind and that I'd like to ask you, as you should be in a good place to answer it. I've wanted to ask you since I was ill. I decided when I was discharged that I'll ask you today.'

'What's it, mama?' she said.

'Mm, you see,' Romoke began, 'the illness I went through was a serious one and which would have claimed my life, but for God's mercy. But then, what does not cease to amaze me is that you doctors treating me couldn't diagnose anything when in actual fact I was not at all well. I know you knew I was ill – in fact, very ill; but your diagnoses kept stating that nothing was wrong with me, till I became actually well. Yemisi, you're a medical doctor; tell me, why was it that your diagnoses kept stating that everything was okay when it was glaring that I was seriously ill?'

Yemisi breathed a sigh.

'Mama,' she began, 'in most cases of this sort, I dare say the illness usually have spiritual basis or cause –I'm telling you this because we are close; no medical practitioner will tell you this in the hospital 'cos the belief is not within medicine. Now, by "spiritual basis or cause",I know you know what I mean. Black magic and the occult are real and are still very much with us today, only that science and technology seem to dominate everywhere now that we may not notice the powers. When an illness is inflicted by the juju powers or the powers we know as "*Aye*[89]" , I'm telling you, we may not be able to

---

89 The Occult

diagnose any illness whatsoever. This is a point where science and technology cannot overrule black magic and the occult.'

'Does it mean', Romoke put in, 'my illness is –'

'Don't conclude yet; I'm not yet through,' Yemisi cut in.

'OK, go on,' said Romoke.

'Now mama,' Yemisi went on, 'I guess there's another possibility for the spiritual cause of such sort of illnesses apart from the black arts'

'What other?' queried Romoke.

'Okay,' continued Yemisi; 'we believe God sometimes tries His people's faith, don't we? And so, He might allow, for instance, a strange illness in a person's body for a period of time – just like the Biblical Job's case. Also, we believe God sometimes judges people's sin by illnesses or diseases like He punished the Israelites for their disobedience by allowing them to be bitten by strange snakes in the Bible. But we do know they are all for a good purpose. But mind you, all these are spiritual and by no means medical!'

Romoke sighed. It was as though she was realising something that she hadn't before. 'Oh, I see!' she said.

'What's that, Mum?' asked Funso.

Romoke then told the story of how her mother Segilola had told her to tell Funso the true account of his paternity and how she had thrown him away, telling her that if she failed to tell him, she might not live to see his good. She concluded, then, that she believed that it was her disobedience to tell Funso what her mother had asked her to tell him that was the cause of her strange illness.

'Mum, do you also know',Funso chipped in, 'that if you hadn't taken ill and hadn't been admitted in that hospital, I wouldn't have met today my dear Yemisi!?'

Yemisi and Romoke laughed.

'But isn't it true, uh?' queried Funso with a rather serious look.

'Actually, it is; oh yes!' replied Romoke. 'Really, everything had worked together for the good of all of us!'she remarked.

* * *

Yemisi and Romoke, together with Funso, were in is the latter's house in the afternoon of that Sunday when Yemisi's father would be visiting. They were sitting in the living room conversing, as they waited for Mr. Olorunsanmi. Soon, Yemisi's phone rang. She took up the call. It was her father calling. He asked for the direction to Funso's place, as he was about to leave the venue of the programme he had come for in Iga. Yemisi gave him the direction and told him she would go to wait for him at the junction of the street to the house. After the conversation, she went to wait for him there.

After about twenty minutes when Yemisi had gone to meet her father, Funso and Romoke heard the gatekeeper open the gate and heard the sound of a car driving in.

'He has come,' said Funso, going to the window to look. 'You wait here Mum,' he said to Romoke as he went to the door.

The car was a black four wheel drive and of automatic transmission. After it was parked, Yemisi and her father came down. Mr. Olorunsanmi had driven the car himself.

Mr. Olorunsanmi was a huge man, tall and fat. He was in his early fifties. He was dressed in a white agbada. He had on a pair of glasses with a grey tint and had on a big chain wristwatch. He was dark and he had a slight pot belly. Mr. Olorunsanmi was a well-to-do cloth dealer.

With the aid of a walking stick, he walked with a slight limp, while Yemisi helped him with his handbag, just for more convenience although of little need.

As Funso was coming out to meet them, they met at the

porch.

'Ah, you're most welcome sir!' beamed Funso, bending forward to touch the tip of a hand to the ground.

'Oh, how do you do?' said Mr. Olorunsanmi, shaking his hand.

'How do you do, sir?' smiled Funso.

Mr. Olorunsanmi turned to Yemisi. 'This is the young man, right?' he whispered.

'Oh yes,' replied Yemisi with a smile –'that's Funso you've been eager to see!'

'Oh, my son-in-law-to-be!' Mr. Olorunsanmi beamed as he embraced him.

Then he turned again to Yemisi and whispered something into her ears. Yemisi laughed aloud.

'You know what?' she said to Funso. 'Dad has seen you in his dream before, so he says he recognizes you at sight!'

Ha, that's great!' Funso chuckled.

'Dad, you're a great seer o!' Yemisi joked.

'If you say so!' Mr. Olorunsanmi chuckled, and they laughed. 'All right, that's enough. Let's go in,' he said, stilling the laughter.

They went inside, Funso leading the way. They got to the living room, and Romoke stood up to welcome Yemisi's father. They exchanged pleasantries with some sort of excitement and Mr. Olorunsanmi was given a warm welcome.

Then they sat down and began conversing. Yemisi went in and brought a bottle of chilled non-alcoholic wine and served her father – their honoured guest, as it were. Then she took her seat. Funso and Yemisi were sitting together on a two-seater sofa facing the plasma TV in the living room. To the left of the two-seater sofa and right beside it was Romoke seated on an armchair, while Mr. Olorunsanmi was sitting at a right angle to her on an armchair.

'It's a great pleasure meeting you, madam,' smiled Mr. Olorunsanmi. 'Actually, Yemisi told me of how you've always been there to give her moral and spiritual advice. And it is my delight that you're not only going to be a mother figure to her now, but you're in fact going to be her mother-in-law!'

'Thank you, Mr. Olorunsanmi,' replied Romoke. 'I also want to use this opportunity to thank you for being willing to give your daughter in marriage to my son – we really appreciate this sir.'

'We should give all thanks to God,' Mr. Olorunsanmi replied and paused. He removed his pair of glasses and put it on the stool beside him, and then he adjusted his sitting posture.

'Now,' he continued with greater enthusiasm, 'let's begin the preparations for their marriage – I mean, let's discuss about fixing the dates for the Introduction and the Engagement ceremonies, and the wedding...'

Romoke's look had changed. It seemed she was discovering something. She was not responding anymore, although Mr. Olorunsanmi didn't take note of the change in her attitude and so continued enthusiastically. Funso and Yemisi were however carried along in the discussion and were contributing with enthusiasm. Romoke kept mute as she rested her chin on her palm and rested the elbow on the arm of her chair; and she was looking straight at Mr. Olorunsanmi with a frown on her face, although he was oblivious of it. Romoke's expression grew bitterer as she looked at him more intently.

Am I dreaming? Or are my eyes deceiving me? But I'm not asleep – I'm very much conscious of my surroundings! Oh God! What a terrible, dangerous play of fate!

'Mum, you ain't contributing,' said Funso, obliviously interrupting Romoke's thoughts.

He noticed the grave, bitter look on his mother's face.

Before he could say anything further, Romoke spoke – in a subdued voice. 'Kindly excuse me; I want to use the toilet.'

She stood up and headed towards the toilet while Funso, who was suspecting that something was wrong, followed her with his gaze till she went out of the living room and into the toilet.

Romoke entered the toilet and shut the door behind her, and then locked it. She rested her back on the door and let out a deep, heavy sigh.

'God, what is this!?'

Her mind went into a series of heart-rending recollections. She shut her eyes firmly, but she could still see his eyes staring back at her. She opened her eyes immediately; but she had had an indelible mark left in her once before which appeared as fresh now as it had been at the beginning of the whole thing. It was as if the deep scar of her hurt was cut opened and oh, bitterness and hatred surged out like blood from a bleeding gash!

'Hmm! This is a terrible play of fate!' she said in a subdued, tremulous voice.

By this time, her brow was covered with sweat and her body was slightly trembling. She again tried to be sure she wasn't dreaming, and each time she tried to be herself she saw that it was stark reality.

What will I do now? This is the most terrible moment so far in my life!

'Mm, I know what I will do!' she muttered.

She paused awhile and then looked straight ahead of her, at nothing in particular, and she spoke in a low, deep angry voice and with a wild look in her eyes.

'The stage is set; the battle trumpet is blown: it is a fight to the finish!'

And with that, she breathed a deep sigh to calm her and

then opened the door, went out and banged the door behind her.

She went back to her seat in the living room. Mr. Olorunsanmi turned to her.

'Yes, madam,' he began, 'we've discussed a few things in your absence and I'll briefly go over them again. Now, the first thing we deliberated on while you were away –'

'Francis Alantakun!' Romoke growled, interrupting.

Mr. Olorunsanmi was transfixed. He took up his pair of glasses and put them on again. He adjusted it and looked carefully at Romoke, and he was just trying to figure out what was actually happening when Romoke growled again.

'I am Romoke Bayetiri! Are you not Francis? YOU AGAIN?'

'My God!' Mr. Olorunsanmi exclaimed, and then he sank to his knees. 'Romoke, please, forgive… forgive my past, I beg of you!'

Yemisi and Funso were lost. They looked at each other, and then each at his or her parent. It seemed a dream to them. Oh poor children!

'You'd better rise to your seat Francis, as your plea can't move me!' roared Romoke.

Mr. Olorunsanmi, who indeed was the man we had known as Francis Alantakun, got up and sat down abashed. Yemisi and Funso felt awkward at the embarrassing situation.

'Now Romoke,' continued Mr. Olorunsanmi, 'I know I don't deserve to be pardoned by you, but please –'

'I beg of you, save me the agony of hearing your plea for pardon!' interrupted Romoke.

Funso turned to Romoke.

'Mum, what's happening here? Am I dreaming? Answer me, Mum! What's happening, please?'

Yemisi went to her father and spoke amidst tears. 'Dad please, explain everything to me – please, Dad!'

'Don't worry, my dear; stop crying,' Mr. Olorunsanmi said in a low voice.

Yemisi was not satisfied. She went over to Romoke. 'Mama, you know I'd come to take you as a mother. You know I told you that as motherless child I didn't find the comfort of a mother anywhere till I met you and found it in you. You know you never denied me any counsel or anything needful for me. Please tell me mama – what's happening?'

Romoke sighed and then paused. Mr. Olorunsanmi's brow was now glistening with beads of sweat.

'Speak mama, please!' begged Yemisi.

'Hmm, the story I told you that day, Yemisi,' Romoke began, 'about a man who seduced me on campus and impregnated me –'

'Please, Romoke – please stop!' Mr. Olorunsanmi cut in.

'And that the man got me to abort the pregnancy,' continued Romoke, 'as a result of which I lost my womb –'

'I beg of you, Romoke –' Mr. Olorunsanmi attempted again.

'Uh-huh? Go on, mama!' said Yemisi, interrupting her father, and slightly shivering as she could hardly bear to hear the next words.

'The man is that man sitting there!' concluded Romoke, pointing straight at Mr. Francis Olorunsanmi.

There was a dead silence!

Yemisi and Funso looked at each other simultaneously, and then at Mr. Olorunsanmi, also at the same time. Then they both began to tremble, again at the same time.

'It's all over!' Mr. Olorunsanmi said under his breath. 'Come Yemisi, let's go,' he said in a weak voice, beckoning to Yemisi.

Yemisi looked at her father, and then at Funso, and then again at her father. 'Go where, Dad? We ain't going nowhere! Let's stay!'

Then she turned to Romoke. 'Mama, but please –'

'My dear,' Romoke interrupted, speaking in a subdued voice heightening with time, 'do you know the weight of what your father did to me? He ruined my life, but only God took it up again and made something good out of it! Your father made me terminate my pregnancy, which caused a serious damage to my womb, and so it had to be removed. He made me lose the foetus which should have been my second child if it was born. Heavens, he made me lose my womb! He made me lose my hope of having any other child. He made me lose the possibility of getting married – and so, I have become and remained a "wombless" single mother of one!'

Mr. Olorunsanmi went on his knees, with tears gathering in his eyes, and he begged, it seemed from the bottom of his heart. 'Romoke, I know I have really hurt you. I know I don't deserve to be pardoned by you – not in the least. I know –'

'You know!' roared Romoke, interrupting. 'Thank God you know! Thank God you realise! You are now sorry after you've ruined me, after you've rendered me without a womb, uh? And you think I will be pacified, with all you did to me? Never! Francis, I beg you, don't try to appease me. As a matter of fact, there's nothing on earth you can do to placate me!'

Mr. Olorunsanmi got up and sat down, and wiped a tear from his eyes with his handkerchief.

'Come Francis,' flared Romoke, 'do you think you could mess up my life and now come to pacify me with entreaties? It's high time you knew you can't go scot-free! You won't get away with it for sure!'

'Romoke, listen –' attempted Mr.Olorunsanmi.

'If you think', continued Romoke, 'you could outsmart

me, you are mistaken! Look, I am disposed to see that you suffer for the hurt you have caused me –'

'Please, listen to me, Romoke –' Mr.Olorunsanmi attempted again.

'Look, you've made a "wombless" woman of me; it is in a more painful and hurting way God will repay you!'

'Romoke please, I beg you by the living God –' Mr.Olorunsanmi attempted yet again.

'God! Do you know God?' mocked Romoke. She burst into a scornful laughter. 'Ha! Ha! What does a brute as you know about God? Ha! You think you can get me to forgive by that, after everything you did to me?'

Now, the contretemps had reached its full height. Yemisi felt very terrible and awkward at the embarrassing situation. Funso was disturbed. They couldn't calm Romoke and Francis. It seemed all efforts to calm the situation rather intensified it, like a bowl of water poured on a raging inferno. They just stood there trembling. Oh, it was really an embarrassing disagreement!

'Romoke, please listen to what I have to say,' begged Mr. Olorunsanmi. 'I know I don't deserve your pardon, but perhaps if you listen to the story of my life since I packed my loads and ran away from campus, when the whole thing happened in 1981 – perhaps if you listen to my story, you might find it in your heart to forgive me. Please, listen to what I have to say.'

'What do you have to say!' flared Romoke. 'I'll hear none of your explanations! None of your excuses! I've had enough of you!'

Mr. Olorunsanmi smiled slightly and spoke in a soft voice.

'The elders say, "If the eye calms down, it will see the nose": Romoke, if you calm down and listen to me, you will see that I did not escape nemesis and perhaps also see why you could forgive me.'

'No! I don't want to hear!' Romoke shouted.

'Mum, you should at least listen to him,' Funso admonished.

Romoke became rather calm.

'OK, speak on; I'm all ears.'

8

Never Again

In a police cell in Ikaodǫgba town on one particular night in July 1981, you could see the figure of a man with each hand clutching on the bars of the cell and with the head bowed.

The man raised his head.

'But why is everything testifying against me?' he said ruefully.'Why is every situation working to bring me misfortunes? God, why not have pity on me and help me, please? I'm completely innocent, and you know!'

And then, he sat on the cold floor of the cell, and after a long while of thinking worriedly he slept off.

Soon after he had slept off, a police officer with a big fat man came to him.

'Francis! Francis Alantakun! Please get up!' the man called.

It was his call that woke up the man in the cell, who was actually Francis Alantakun. The big fat man, who was Francis' boss, ordered for him to be released from the detention.

And he said to him, 'We're very sorry. We now have the

correct information and the true picture of the whole thing!'

Actually, Francis had been working under this man, his boss, in his big cloth shop, as a clerk, and he had been working since the month before, that is, June. He had always been diligent in his work and he had been loyal to his boss. He had a personal ambition, to be a successful cloth dealer and he always came alive each time he talked about it.

It then happened that one day, when his boss had booked for seven hundred bundles of a cloth from a wholesaler that the goods had then been delivered to them. Francis had been in-charge of receiving the goods. He had received the goods at their own store; but he had been so occupied that he couldn't count them himself, so he had sent someone under him to do the counting. This person who he assigned to count the goods however made some counting errors, somehow, and counted everything to be seven hundred bundles when in actual fact six hundred bundles were delivered; but Francis recorded seven hundred bundles of the cloth delivered.

Meanwhile, the time Francis had slated for him to resign and opt for his own cloth trade was up, although he was oblivious to the counting error concerning the goods delivered to his boss. It was a costly coincidence! The day that followed that day that the goods were delivered, Francis had handed his resignation to his boss. The latter was about to dismiss the former when he had a need to go to the store. When he got there, he had to count the delivered goods. He also made Francis to count them. Francis was most baffled at what he counted the bundles to be! There was no soap he could use to wash his hands clean of the allegation of theft. Nobodyexcept Godwas his witness that he actually had not stolen the remaining hundred bundles. Everything testified against him. His resignation did. His ambition to be a prosperous cloth dealer which he had never ceased to talk about testified against him. His position of being in-charge of the goods as well did.Only God knew he was innocent!

However, after Francis had remained in police custody for

two days, the truth of the whole situation had been discovered. The person whom Francis' boss had booked the seven hundred bundles with had come to the latter. He had then explained to him that the error had been on the part of his own errand boys; that they had mistakenly delivered six hundred bundles instead of the seven hundred he had booked for. He had therefore sent the remaining one hundred bundles to him.

Now, Francis' boss explained everything to him at the police station and begged him not to take offence at all that happened. He also compensated him with a considerable sum of money.

Francis then went home. On arriving at the doorstep, he noticed everywhere was unduly silent. He saw a young man dressed casually in T-shirt and trousers in front of the house. He wondered what he was up to, just standing there.

'Hello, can I help you?' Francis said.

'I want to see the daddy in the house and I don't know if anybody is in? Can you help me... please?' he said, pronouncing his words one by one.

What sort of a moron is this one? Francis thought; for the man was behaving imbecile *as he spoke. Anyway, let me help him; maybe he's sick in the head.*

Francis took him in, leading the way; but as he opened the door and entered in first, lo and behold, two hands pointed a pistol each at each side of his head. He saw his father with the four wives and also his siblings lying prostrate on the floor. The man whom Francis was leading in, on ensuring that he had entered the house, closed the door on him, and continued his 'guarding work' outside. It was then that Francis knew he had come to meet armed robbers in operation.

'Hands up!' the gang leader ordered, and they collected all the money on him. When they discovered he was part of the family, they ordered him to lead them to where they had their money kept. He hesitated, and they gave him some hard beatings; and then on his own, he led them there.

The robbers ransacked the house and brought out their valuables. And then, the gang leader announced, '*Hey, na Phase 1 be dat! We don come Phase 2!* [91]' Then he ordered, '*Girls, comot ya clothes now! You no hear word!!? A' say –* [92]'

Unspeakable fear took hold of Francis and he broke out in cold sweat.

'Please, I beg you, spare them!' he begged, his voice quivering. 'I'll give you whatever you demand from me, please! You can do whatever you like to me, just don't kill me, I beg you! Please... please, spare my sisters, I beg you!'

'*Aha! Boys o, make we deal wit dis one first! He wan form saviour shey? mouna leave di babes for now!* [93]' one of the robbers said.

Two of them descended on Francis and punched him hard. After then he lay on the floor weak and groaning in pains. Then they dragged him into one room and locked him up. They also took his father and the other boys there and locked them all up.

'*I go count from one to seven! If I reach seven you no comot ya clothes I go gun una one time – I swear!* [94]' the gang leader shouted.

Francis could not contain it where he was. He began to yell out and to bang on the door.

His sisters and half-sisters cried and begged, trembling.

The gang leader began the count.

'One!

'Two!

'Three!'

'Four –'

---

91 (Pidgin English) All that is Phase 1! Time for Phase Two 2 now!
92 Girls, take off your clothes now! Don't you hear me! I say –
93 (Pidgin English) Aha! Boys, let's deal with this one first! He wants to prove a saviour? You leave the babes for now!
94 I'll count one to seven! If by seven you've not taken off your clothes, I'll gun you down – I swear!

Suddenly the police siren was heard wailing and getting closer and closer. They rushed out, leaving behind the valuables, but they took along all the money. They all escaped before the police got there. One of Francis' sisters went to open the door for him and the others.

She put her hand in Francis', looked up at him with tears glistening in her eyes, and said, 'Ah, Brother, thank you! If not for you – I can't imagine what would have happened. Thank you, big bro.'

'My pleasure, dear,' replied Francis, his voice still trembling. 'Thank God they didn't touch you. Thank God they didn't!'

After they had all calmed down a little, Francis told them how he was released from detention. And later at about nine thirty that evening, he went to the house of one of his friends. And when he was yet some distance away from the house, he saw the friend, who had been sitting outside, rushing inside. When he got there and asked of him, someone came out and told him that he was not in. Francis asserted that he saw him just then, but the person replied that it was just then that he went out; and Francis, suspecting that he was not welcomed there, turned around and left.

He went to another friend of his who was aware of his being in police custody; and he told him of his release and also of the armed robbery attack, hoping to get words of consolation and encouragement as well as some amount of money from him, that he might be solaced at least. But then, what he got he least expected it.

His friend told him that the fact that he had a misfortune following another – the fact that as he escaped one he got into another – testified to the hard fact that he had an ill luck. He told him that his head – the body part believed to be the symbol of a person's luck and fortune – was bad and needed to be 'washed', and that till then, he might not cease to have a line of mishaps and misfortunes. He told him, moreover, that the saddest thing about it was that the ill fortune was contagious. He added that it was a risk that he his friend was taking to continue to befriend him, as he also might be 'infected' with Francis' bad luck. He however said that it was because he loved Francis that he was telling him all that; and that if he didn't love him he would have kept it from him and only be avoiding him. He then concluded that so that things might be safe for both of them, Francis should try to keep his distance from him, until he (that is, Francis) had gone for a spiritual head-wash!

Francis was not in the least solaced but rather was disheartened. *If this is what friendship is – to love you only when things go well with you, then to hell with it! To hell with it!*

His friend gave him quite some amount of money and then said good night.

Francis left and headed for a pub in the town,. He went with a view to finding solace in high quality exotic beer and drive away worry with it, at least for the moment.

Francis got to the pub and entered the lounge bar. There was revelry in the air. Youths as well as the old were all carried away with the merrymaking. You could see old men of some eminence – the sugar daddies – sitting in the bar room with cute young girls, the'sweet-sixteen's'! Likewise you could see the big boys with girls of their age groups all around them, like tsetse flies besiege Fulani cattle! You could hardly see a man in that place, without seeing at least a lady –his inamorata – with him!

After Francis had ordered himself a beer, he sat alone at a corner in the barroom. He rested his chin on the palm of his left hand and rested the elbow on the table – a posture that suggested that he was thinking worriedly. He took a sip from his beer mug from time to time, and time and again he let out sighs of worry.

Francis didn't know that he was being watched keenly by somebody. Who would have interest in him? (he might have thought.) After all, the bar was too lively and full of merrymaking for anyone to have time to think of his sombre person. Besides, he was mean; and the lounge bar was full of well-to-do people.

He had then finished the bottle and he was hanging his head, still dejected. It seemed the worry was too strong to be conquered at once by one bottle. He was thinking of going for one more – but the cost of that exotic brand was not a joking matter! He hung his head. He knew quite well that he would soon forget the worries when the alcohol now takes over the lordship of his system; but then, it would be a momentary ease from worries, for they would still come again after the influence of the alcohol on him.

While he hung his head he heard someone called over him. 'Hallo!'

He looked up and saw a sexy young lady of twenty-four. Short-curly-haired. Small-statured and slim-bodied. Light-complexioned. She had on a pair of gold dangly earrings, her wrist adorned with gold bangles; and she was cutely dressed and had her feet attractively shod. She was slightly bending over him.

'How are you?'

Francis feigned a smile.

'Fine,' he said. Then he added, 'Thanks.'

'I'm Felicia,' she said. 'Can I have my seat?'

'Oh, sure!' said Francis, gesturing to her to take her seat in front of him. 'And my name is Francis.' He shook her hand. 'Pleased to meet you,' he said.

'The pleasure is mine,' replied Felicia and then paused a bit. 'I've been watching you all along and I noticed you sat all alone and perhaps dejected. Is anything the matter, if I may ask?'

Francis breathed a sigh.

'Felicia, there are problems! I've seen big problems in the past few days! It is to discard my worries that I turn to the bottle.'

'Mm, do you mind sharing them, perhaps I may be of help?' said Felicia, with a gleam of affection and concern in her eyes.

'I don't mind,' replied Francis.

'All right – Now, do you want us to go outside, to one of the huts, for some solitude?' asked Felicia.

'It's okay – that'd be better,' remarked Francis.

They went to one of the wooden huts around the pub. Francis started to tell Felicia what had befallen him, from how he was wrongly accused of theft in his working place to his detention, to the robbery attack and to how his friends were now avoiding him.

'I'm fed up with life itself!' he concluded. 'What is left of your worth if your close friends now see you as someone to run away from; as someone to be avoided; as someone not to be associated with; as someone not in the least better than an outcast!' he blurted in the peak of dejection.

Francis' words had really tugged at Felicia's heartstrings.

'Francis, I'll… I'll be your friend,' she said to him softly, sweetly, soothingly.

He stared in disbelief.

'You mean you'll stand by me despite all these!' he gasped.

Felicia nodded.

He took her hands in his, squeezing them gently, as tears welled up in his eyes. 'Thank you, Felicia. Thank you so much,' he said, extremely solaced.

At that point a young lady ran to the hut and peeped inside. 'Felicia, we've been… looking for – oh, you're having a date!'

'Will you behave for a moment!' shouted Felicia, reproving her friend with whom, together with some other two, she had come to the pub. 'You guys don't know anything other than, dating!'

'Shut up!' the friend shouted jokingly. 'In any case, I just want to tell you we're leaving!'

'You guys go, I'm not a kid; I don't have to follow you!' said Felicia.

'Oh, I wouldn't want to keep you behind unduly,' Francis said politely.

'No, never mind,' Felicia replied.

'Oh, I'm jealous o!' the friend joked as she left.

* * *

Francis and Felicia became close friends. They went almost everywhere together. They did things together. They were lovebirds.

As days passed, their friendship grew into a romantic relationship. They both fell in love with each other. For the first time, Francis was truly in love! This time around it wasn't lust, or infatuation – our man was in love with a girl! Francis came to adore Felicia so much that he could do anything for her. She had stolen his heart and he wouldn't get it back! He couldn't contemplate what life would be like if he lost her. It was too bitter to imagine for him. If you would really move Francis, you could tell him Felicia lay sick in the hospital. And if you would make him feel very terrible, you could tell him she was no longer interested in the relationship! Really, Felicia was more than the world to him; she was simply the love of his life!

At many times, they spent the night together in bed. On one of those nights, after sex, Felicia told Francis that she'd got a piece of good news for him.

'Good news! Oh tell me!' said an anxious Francis.

'Guess what!' smiled Felicia.

'You know I'm not good at guessing.'

'Just try; guess it.'

'What if I guess wrong?'

'Try!'

Francis paused, trying to guess. Then he spoke at once. 'You've got a job!'

'Nope!'

'You won the lottery!'

'Nope!'

'Then tell me!'

'OK, place your hand here on my tummy,' said Felicia.

Francis placed his hand on her belly and wondered what she was about doing or saying.

Felicia smiled and spoke calmly. 'Junior has got there!'

Francis sprung back. 'What does that mean?'

'Francis, I'm pregnant!' beamed Felicia.

'What!' he exclaimed, rather taken aback.

'You shocked? Ain't you happy? Ain't you expecting it?'

He didn't answer. He just stared.

'Huh? I'm talking to you!' Felicia shouted.

'Actually… actually…I wasn't expecting it,' said Francis.

'But you must prepare to take care of it now that it has come, uh?' said Felicia.

Francis breathed a sigh and nodded.

'Uh-huh… I agree. I agree.'

'I'd been telling you for quite some time now about the issue of us getting married soon, but you've always said we should still continue this way; that we could always get wedded anytime later on –say this time next year, you said. But Francis, don't you think it's high time we gave it a real thought?' queried Felicia.

Francis breathed a sigh. 'It's true; but I fear, the church

may not want to conduct the marriage for us now that you're pregnant before marriage.'

Felicia laughed.

'The church I attend', she said, 'is one that is less concerned about whether the couple to be joined had pre-marital sex or not. Look, it was in those days chastity is considered one priceless thing; today, even bishops' daughters abort several times before they go to the altar! And everything is "Holy Matrimony"! Ha! Even if the church can't conduct it, we can have a court wedding, can't we?'

'Oh, that's true – I didn't even think of that!' said Francis.

'But don't worry yourself, Francis; my priest will not refuse to conduct the marriage – we'll have a white wedding! Just relax!' said Felicia.

And then they went on another round of sexual intercourse.

* * *

Now it was May 1982 and the month was at its end. Francis and Felicia had been wedded for seven months then, for they got wedded in November 1981. Now, Felicia was to be delivered of a baby and she was in the labour room of The General Hospital, in Ikaodọgba –the same town where they settled after their wedding.

It was the morning of that Saturday, and Felicia had been in labour for about eight hours already. She had exhausted her strength to 'push'. Francis was not himself again where he was outside the delivery room. He couldn't keep calm or keep still; he kept pacing up and down anxiously.

Then at once, the doctor that was in charge of the delivery came out of the delivery room. Francis immediately rushed to him. 'Doctor... Doctor! How's she?'

'Calm down, Mr.Alantakun,' the doctor said calmly. 'Come,' he then said, beckoning at him as he headed towards his surgery.

At his sugery, the doctor told Francis that her wife would have to go through a Caesarean straight away. Francis was troubled and was apprehensive. The doctor encouraged him that all was going to be well.

The Caesarean was conducted and it was successful. And a baby girl was delivered by it. Francis was overjoyed. But then, his joy was soon subdued and distress took over, for Felicia after the successful Caesarean developed some complications as a result of haemorrhage; and then she lay weak on the hospital bed.

Francis sat by her, consoling her, hoping she would soon get well. He took her hand. 'You'll soon get well,' he said.

'Thank you, dear; I pray so,' Felicia replied in a weak voice, her face wan. 'But my dear,' she added, 'I'm quite apprehensive. I'm afraid I may die.'

'No... no you won't die – God will preserve you for me; no you won't die!' Francis said, his voice shaking slightly.

He paused awhile, tears gathering in his eyes; and he spoke feelingly. 'Look Felicia, I wish it is me who suffers this – if at all possible – and not you! Look, I've done bad things in life! I'd led a wayward life before I met you – I deserve this, not you poor innocent soul!'

'Don't say that – everybody has a certain bad past that hunts them,' remarked Felicia.

'But mine is so awful that I won't be pleased that it should be you that'll suffer the consequences of it,' said Francis.

He paused a bit and then continued.

'When I was on campus, I led a rather immoral life. I see girls as means, means to satisfy my sexual urges. I descend on them anytime I just feel like having it. Mm, but there was this girl I can't forget! I seduced her, succeeded, got her pregnant, got her to abort the pregnancy; and then she lost her womb as a result of it!'

'Ha!' exclaimed Felicia.

'But I faced misfortunes – because of her, I believe,' said Francis. 'But why should I bring my own misfortune on you for Heaven's sake?' he blurted.

'Ha Francis, don't think I don't also have a bad past, as bad as yours too!' said Felicia. 'I too once led an immoral life – in fact, a promiscuous one!'

'Huh!' exclaimed Francis in disbelief.

'Uh-huh! I had boyfriends more than my fingers can count, and having sex with them was almost a daily affair, if I will not exaggerate!' said Felicia.

Francis was taken aback but he restrained himself from showing too much surprise. He tried to keep calm and listen.

'You met me', continued Felicia, 'as Miss Felicia Ayelangbe, but I was not at all a virgin – I'd lost it since I was thirteen! And I took it on myself to motivate other girls to have it too. I'd introduced far too many innocent girls into sex, masturbation and even lesbianism, and almost all of them got addicted!'

'Ha!' exclaimed Francis.

Now, it was from Felicia's words that we come to know that her maiden name was Ayelangbe.

'But I can't just forget one of them,' continued Felicia – 'the reason why, I can't really tell. I met her when I went to retake in her school in the '70's. She was a devoted Christian and was so innocent; but I corrupted her. By the time I left that town, I'd succeeded in making her addicted to sex. She had had sex with nine boys or so on many occasions!'

'HA!!' exclaimed Francis.

Felicia dissolved into tears. 'Look, I deserve what now happens to me! I deserve it in every way!' she sobbed.

Francis held her hands and squeezed them, to solace her, but tears ran down his own eyes too. Oh, they were both haunted by guilt! The thoughts of their bad past struck the hearts of them both like a dart. Their hearts were stricken by guilt deep and unbearable! Too deeply felt to be expressed in words!

Then at once, Francis sprang up from beside Felicia. He rushed to a nurse who was at some distance from where Felicia lay on her sick bed. 'Please Nurse, what… what is today's date?' he asked with great anxiety, nervousness and apprehension.

'Erm, today's date is twenty-ninth of May,' the nurse replied.

'My God!' Francis burst out, laying his two hands on his head, signifying misfortune.

'What's the matter, Mr. Man?' the nurse asked.

Francis did not answer. He walked slowly back to Felicia with his hands on his head still and with his mouth open.

'Come, Mr. Man, what's the problem?' the nurse asked, but he did not respond.

Francis had just remembered that it was exactly a year before then that he got Romoke to abort her pregnancy that she had for him and which she aborted on that same date and also got her womb removed on that same date – May the twenty-ninth 1981! Now, it was another May the twenty-ninth, exactly a year after the fateful incident. Francis had thought he had got away with how he had brutalised Romoke. But now, nemesis had caught up with him!

'Ah, please God let nemesis not come on me in this point – my wife's life! She's all I have! Ah, that would really hit me where it hurts! No please! No please!' he blurted pleadingly, in a subdued voice, and began to sweat profusely.

Just as he was going to Felicia, another nurse entered. 'Mr. Francis Alantakun!' she called him.

'Yes, Nurse? What's it?' he replied, anxious.

'The doctor wants to see you,' she said.

'The doctor!' he exclaimed and then dashed out at once and headed for his surgery, walking very fast.

The doctor told Francis that his wife had got some complications as a result of an acute haemorrhage and that she might not likely survive it, as they might lose her in less than an hour – that is, she had less than an hour to live, according to him. And he tried to brace him for the unfortunate thing that might happen anytime from then.

'No, she can't die! No, please!' Francis burst out, banging his fist on the desk.

He got up, sweating, and rushed to see Felicia again. The doctor followed him. On their way, the nurse that was with Felicia met them. She was panting.

'What happened?' the doctor asked.

'It's… it's the woman – the woman that gave birth this morning!' the nurse said, painting.

'Uh, my Felicia!?' exclaimed Francis.

'Uh-huh, what happened to her?' the doctor enquired.

'She… she… she just –' the nurse hesitated.

'OK, let's go there,' the doctor said.

They went to Felicia, but lo and behold, she lay on the bed absolutely motionless, her eyes shut and her body gradually growing cold! Francis was shocked to his very bones.

'What actually happened?' the doctor enquired from the nurse.

'She… she was praying and crying,' the nurse began; 'she was making confessions. I told her she needed to rest, but she begged that she dearly needed to pray and that I should allow her just some minutes. After a while of prayer, she started to sing; and soon after, to my surprise, she began to gasp. Before I knew it, sir, she… she stopped breathing!'

'Yeh! My God!' exclaimed Francis, laying his hands on his head, and then covering his face with his two palms, in dread.

The doctor took his stethoscope and listened to her heartbeat, but he could not hear the throb, for it had ceased! He turned to Francis, who was looking intently at him.

'I'm sorry,' he said – 'we've lost her!'

Francis grabbed his head with his two hands. His eyeballs went red and he broke out in a cold sweat. The words 'I'm sorry – we've lost her!'seemed to echo in his ears over and over again. His head at once began to ache. His eyes went dim for some seconds, and he could only see things vaguely for that first moment of the shock.

'Aargh!!!' he burst out as he sunk to his knees. 'My whole world is turned upside down!'

* * *

The week following the loss of his wife, Francis was not himself again. That he had a baby was not even enough to solace him. It was mixed feelings for him. He could not celebrate just because of a child born to him, when he had lost his wife – someonevery dear to his heart; and he could not so much weep because of the death of his wife, when he had got a baby – a gift from God. Mixed feelings it really was for him.

On Monday, the last day of that month May, Francis' mother Mrs. Alantakun, was beside him in his house. She was so bothered about how he was having too much emotional distress on the issue. It had been two days now since he lost Felicia and he hadn't tasted anything called food or really slept.

'Please Francis, ọkọ mi [95], eat something,' the mother begged.

It is needful to say here that in Yourba land, mothers do sometimes call their son, or daughter, 'ọkọ mi' – that is, 'my husband' – especially when pleading with them, to show affection.

Now, Francis did not respond. He kept staring as though it wasn't him she was talking to.

'Why, you'll kill yourself this way, my son!' the mother

---

95 My husband; my darling.

shouted at once. 'Why are you behaving as if the worst thing that can happen to a person has happened to you? Can't you thank God that you have a baby? Is that not enough? Must you kill yourself for Heaven's sake?' she queried. Then her voice dropped. 'But Francis, this is the second day now that you haven't taken anything, and you've not yet rested. Why, uh? At least, take a little food and rest, uh?'

'Mama, sorrow will not allow a morsel to enter my mouth or allow my eyes to close and sleep,' replied Francis matter-of-factly; 'but let me make an attempt, perhaps hunger will triumph over loss of appetite,' he added.

His mother prepared ẹba and okro soup and served him. And when he took a few morsels of the ẹba, he couldn't continue any further, for he lacked appetite.

Then after he had washed his hand (for the bare hand is used to eat the food in Yoruba culture), he turned to his mother and queried, 'But Mama, why are misfortunes happening to me? Have I been born with misfortunes,uh?'

'No my son; don't think like that,' his mother said.

'OK mama; let me ask you this question.'

'What is it, my son?'

'Mama, why is it that my weakness "is ladies", from the very outset?'

'Why do you ask?'

'Answer my question mama!'

'Ah, I don't seem to know.'

'You don't seem to know? OK, why is our family name "Alantakun", that means "Spider"?'

'That, I'm not in the best place to answer; ask your father!' the mother replied.

'You don't seem to know that too? OK, why is my father a womanizer– having four wives and three mistresses – why?' Francis demanded.

'Don't call your father a womanizer, son!' the mother reproved.

'OK, whatever he is – answer my question, mama,' said Francis.

'Ask your father – he will tell you if he is pleased to!' the mother shouted.

'Mama, you'd better answer my question before I force my way to God!' Francis shouted,gripping his neck with his two hands as though ready to snuff out his own life.

The mother immediately got up and, almost kneeling down for him, she begged feelingly as she robbed her palms together back and forth. *'Dakun jo 'o, oko mi⁹⁶* , don't kill yourself. I will pose those questions to your dad and urge him to answer everything – I promise.'

Francis then stopped his simulated attempt to kill himself.

* * *

Francis went from time to time to his older sister's house, who, being a nurse by profession, took it upon herself to look after his baby. Each time Francis looked into the baby's eyes, he felt solaced, at least to some extent.

The eighth day, which traditionally was meant to be the day for the naming of the child, was drawing closer. Meanwhile, the body of Felicia had been buried. Francis, nonetheless, did not cease to mourn her.

On Wednesday, June the second, when his father Mr. Olorunsanmi Alantakun, came to his house to mourn with him, console him and encourage him, Francis demanded that he told him why they bore the family name 'Alantakun' – the Yoruba word for Spider. Mr. Olorunsanmi told him that he couldn't tell him, considering his (that is, Francis') health and promised to tell him sometime later. However, Francis demurred and

---

96 Please and please, my husband.

demanded that he told him there and then. When his father refused, Francis attempted snuffing out his own life again and also told his father that unless he knew all there was to know about their family name, he would certainly not get better.

And so, Mr. Olorunsanmi Alantakun began the story that surrounded the significant family name. And the story he told him went thus.

There once was a great hunter by the name Odejimi in a small Yoruba town called Shagalu in the 1930's, who was a man of great charm (that is, charisma) and was also great and versed in the use of charms (that is, magic spells). He was great but he had a weakness which he was not cognizant of – inordinate love for women! He had eight wives, five concubines and nine mistresses! He was thus hailed and praised as a man, a virile man! Most people didn't know him by his real name Odejimi. He had a nickname which the people of Shagalu gave him for his charm, his charisma, that magnetised to him every beautiful maiden that came across him or he came across, who became transfixed and caught, as it were, in the 'web' of his charm. And hence did the nickname, 'Alantakun' (that is, 'Spider') aptly fit him.

But then, there was one day, Odejimi saw one stunningly beautiful maiden. He attended a festival in one of the neighbouring towns, where some maidens performed traditional cultural dances. They were dressed in traditional attires. They had only wrappers, of *ofi*[97] cloth type, tied around their body, leaving their shoulders and arms bare. They also tied small wrappers of the same *ofi* firmly around their bottoms. They had long traditional necklaces with big beads around their neck and they were bare-footed.

After the whole entertainment, Odejimi approached one of the maidens that danced, for he had fallen in love with her. When he had a chat-up with her, she also lost her heart to him. But then, there was a problem that Abeke – for that was the

_____
97 A type of woven cloth.

name of the young lady – would have to face: she was already betrothed to a young man by the name Shogbemi; however, she had been caught in the web of Odejimi's irresistible charm (that is, his charisma), that she could not but lose all her heart to him! She was then ready to face whatever threat and hostility that could come from Shogbemi, his people and in fact, her own people. She was disposed to go with Odejimi whom her heart now loved come what may.

After the whole festival, and Abeke told her mother of this other man her heart longed for and that she would want to marry him, and in fact go home with him that very day, her mother demurred and wondered what had suddenly come over her girl that she could no longer reason. She told Abeke's father, who at once insisted that she was going nowhere, neither was he going to allow her to marry him. Again, the father had had much about the said Odejimi and wouldn't want her daughter to be married to such a womanizer as him.

Abeke sneaked out to tell Odejimi, who was waiting under a tree in a dark hidden place, that he should come back to take her in two days; that she hoped to have convinced her parents by then.

When on the following day Shogbemi heard of everything and confirmed that it was true, he became sorely disappointed and sad. He became really jealous of his virgin fiancée he had preserved all along for himself. He felt so grieved that he took ill. When his father, who was a renowned traditional occultist in that area and was more expert and experienced in the use of magic spells than Odejimi – when he knew the cause of Shogbemi's melancholic mood, he told him that it wasn't anything difficult. But when he learnt that Alantakun was the man in question, he remarked that the work may prove rather difficult,though not impossible; for he knew Odejimi in the occult to be quite a strong man.

Shogbemi's father then gave him a traditional Yoruba magic charm called 'Magun' with which he carefully gave him specific instructions on how to use it in order to trap Odejimi. He told him that he should lay the charm on the floor at a doorpost that Abeke would immediately after be the first to enter through, and then ensure that Abeke, unaware, crossed over it. The charm was in form of a broomstick and so thin that it couldn't be easily noticed. Shogbemi's father told him that once Abeke crossed over it, she would be under a spell, that whoever had sexual intercourse with her within ninety days after, the person would certainly die: and thus Odejimi would be trapped, unless he wouldn't have an intercourse with Abeke till ninety days elapsed, which Odejimi, being oblivious to the spell, could not but do – that was his weakness! Odejimi could not contain his desire for women, no he could not!

And so it happened that Shogbemi succeeded in making Abeke cross over the magic spell – she being oblivious to it – before she went with Odejimi to his house in Shagalu town.

When the day came that Odejimi would come to take Abeke, Abeke's parents saw that she was in love with Odejimi and they agreed that she go with him. Meanwhile, Odejimi had brought along his bride price and many enticing gifts to the parents. Abeke's parents were so much impressed and proud that their daughter was marrying a great man. And thus did Odejimi succeed in having Abeke as wife that day; and he took him to his house.

On getting to Odejimi's house, Abeke's was shocked when she realised that she had come to face wife rivalries, seeing the so-many women that this man she had given her heart to completely, had. Ah, she was in for it!

When Odejimi ordered one of his concubines to prepare amala with egusi soup for Abeke, his 'new and most beloved wife', the woman became very envious, especially for rating Abeke as dearer to him than all of them who had been his for a good number of years then. When the meal was set, the concubine that prepared it brought it to Abeke and served her, smiling endearingly. Abeke took a liking to her, thinking she must be a well-mannered, tender-hearted woman and that she was going to take her as companion rather than a rival wife.

Meanwhile, Odejimi was in the bathroom which was a little wooden construction like a shed, at the back of the house.

By the time Abeke washed her hands and wanted to take the first morsel of the amala, Odejimi appeared and immediately, stopping Abeke,shouted, '*Agbẹdọ*[98]! ' Then he ordered the concubine who had prepared it to eat it herself.

The latter began to plead and sob,but Odejimi insisted firmly that she must take it herself. She wept sorely, kneeling down, but Odejimi would not listen to her. At a point, he just ordered her to pack all her loads and be gone from his house. She begged so much but no, her pleadings would not move Odejimi. He did send her packing that day!

The food was left there till night. In the night it had completely turned purple as if dyed – a sign that it contained a deadly poison! It was then Abeke knew what the woman had been up to. Fright took hold of her and it dawned on her that she could have died but for the timely intervention of her great husband with knowing ability. This deepened her love for him, which made Odejimi to take her as his favourite among all his wives, concubines and mistresses.

At night while they had intercourse, lo and behold, Odejimi was struck by a strange thunderbolt and turned somersaults, three times – these impact and effect being symptomatic of the *Magun* spell, to result in instant death. Odejimi would have died at that instant when the magical thunderbolt hit him and he completed the three somersaults,if not for his own magical immunity which could withstand to some degree Shogbemi's father's magical powers. But then, the magical impact did leave him paralysed.

Now, as days rolled into weeks and weeks into months, with Odejimi's strange paralysis aggravating and not improving, his wives and concubines started to desert him one by one till they all left him. His sons and daughters also abandoned him. Only Abeke stood by him taking good care of him, after all it was

---

98 Never!

because of her he was suffering.

Meanwhile, Abeke was already pregnant for Odejimi and she was nearing her day of delivery. Abeke promised that even if it happened that Odejimi died, she wasn't going to marry another person; that she had given all her heart to him and no other man would have it. Odejimi also said that if he happened to die, it is to Abeke's child which was in her womb that the larger proportion of his assets and possessions would go. And he already stated how all he had was going to be divided as inheritance for all his children, in the presence of witnesses.

And the day came that Abeke would be delivered of her baby. Her little room with a small wooden window in the quaint thatched mud house was her delivery room, as there were no maternity centres in those days. Two old veteran traditional mid-wives delivered her baby – a bouncing baby boy. And when Odejimi, who was already on his deathbed (for he died thereafter) – when he saw the baby and Abeke his wife, he felt sad that he could only see his baby born, but would not live to see him grow to become a man, as he was going to join his forebears. He lamented that his desire for Abeke had then turned against him to cut his own life short, and that he would not even live to enjoy life with her. He thought that if he had been content with what he had, he wouldn't have had to suffer the strange illness and wouldn't have to die, and Abeke wouldn't have to become a widow. He regretted that what he craved for and desired would now kill him. Of course, he had what he wanted. He desired the beautiful maiden, whom he would do anything to get; and he got his urge satisfied too; but now, he would not live to enjoy life with her again!

Then Odejimi named Abeke's baby 'Ọlọrunsanmi' – a Yoruba name that means 'God repays me' – and soon after Odejimi gave up the ghost. And thus was the child named 'Olorunsanmi, son of Alantakun' – and he grew up to become the father of Francis Alantakun, and who told Francis his son this story.

* * *

Francis, after hearing the full story behind their family name, was just satisfied to have heard it; however, he was not in the least solaced by it. After his father left, he lay down and took a framed picture of Felicia, gazed at it for a long while and laid it over his heart, a tear rolling down his face. And soon he slept off.

Early on the following day, Thursday, Francis' relatives came to his house to plan for the naming ceremony of his baby that would hold on Saturday that week. While they were discussing in the living room with Francis also there, the latter, at some point, asked to be excused, saying that he was feeling weak and would want to go and lie down in the bedroom. As he stood up and just took a few steps, he slumped and went into a coma. Everybody sprang up. His older sister, the nurse examined him and stated that he had gone into a coma and had been partly paralysed with stroke. He was rushed to The General Hospital there in Ikaodọgba town, where he was admitted straight away.

Francis remained in a coma throughout that Thursday and through Friday morning and afternoon. He didn't regain consciousness until Friday evening, he woke up to see his father and mother sitting beside him. 'Where is my baby?' was the first words that came out from his lips, and he spoke in a low, weak voice. The father and mother screamed for joy and called the nurses. The nurses called the doctor.

The doctor examined him and noted that his was improving rather fast. He asked the parents to excuse him as he would need much rest. But then, Francis begged that the doctor allow him to speak to them just for a few minutes. The doctor wouldn't listen but he begged more earnestly and he then gave them just ten minutes to talk.

'How is my baby?'

'She's fine; your sister's taking good care of her,' the mother replied.

He paused and let out deep sigh.

'I deem myself honoured by God to have the baby, despite my wayward life. So I'll name her "*Oluwayẹmisi*[99]".

He paused a little bit and then continued, turning to his father. 'Daddy, I've come to realise from our family story you told me, that my weakness of lust after girls was actually an inherited trait from my grandpa, perhaps reinforced by that significant name "Alantakun". But now, Daddy, no longer will I be a spider, catching every girl that comes across me, catching them in my web! No longer!'

He looked up and prayed, a tear rolling down the side of his face.

'Jesus Christ, merciful Saviour, please forgive my many sins! I've ruined many girls' lives. I've dashed many girls' hopes. And now You've repaid me in a way that has completely broken me down. This really hits me where it hurts! But I beg You, God, please take up my life from its ruin that it is in now and make a beautiful edifice out of it!'

He wiped the tear with his right hand which wasn't paralysed, and then he turned again to his father.

'Daddy, when I looked at my situation and see how God has repaid me, I deem it fit to have your own first name "Olorunsanmi" – "God repays me" – as my own surname from now on; rather than the family name "Alantakun".'

'That's all right; you can!' the father approved.

'So', continued Francis, 'I'll be called "Francis Olorunsanmi" from now on, and my baby's name will be "Yemisi Olorunsanmi". Ah, I'll always mourn my dear wife – I will always mourn her!

'Hm, never again will I be a spider catching every beautiful girl that crosses my path! Never again will I have a predatory attitude to girls! Never again will I ruin any girl's life! NEVER AGAIN! NEVER AGAIN!'

---

99 A Yoruba name meaning 'The Lord honours me'.

9

Reconciled - Together Again

'…And so, I resolved to remain unmarried after her death. Well, that's my story – you've heard it all,' concluded Mr. Francis Olorunsanmi, who had been narrating his story to Romoke all along.

'Felicia Ayelangbe! Heavens!' Romoke exclaimed, staring at nothing in particular.

'What? Did you know her?' asked Francis.

'See nemesis at work!' Romoke exclaimed, still staring and not minding to answer Francis.

'Ah! Is she a relative of yours, or what?' Francis asked further, baffled and rather scared.

'Mum, what's it?' Funso asked too.

She took a deep breath to calm her and then spoke.

'I met her when she came to retake her O'level papers in my secondary school, Odo-Akan Grammar School, and I too was sitting for the exam. It was then I gave birth to Funso premaritally. She was the one who got me into having sex. I threw my baby away then. I threw him away out of despair, but I got him back after I aborted the pregnancy I had for you, just by some coincidence – a divine one, I believe. It's a long story, anyway.'

'Oh, I didn't know all these,' said Francis. 'I never knew you once had a baby before that incident in May 1981; I guess that's why it was difficult for me to guess the "Funso Bayetiri" that proposed to my daughter was actually your own son. I never even linked the name to you in anyway.'

Then his voice dropped as he went on his knees.

'Romoke, you see how I didn't at all escape nemesis, and God forgave my sins and made me a new person. I beg you, forgive me; after all, God also forgives us when we do wrong – please, Romoke.'

Romoke stood up slowly, tears gathering in her eyes, and she spoke with a voice shaking slightly with emotion.

'How easy do you think that would be for me? You rendered me without a womb! You took advantage of me and dumped me! Francis, you deeply hurt me, I must tell you!'

Yemisi stood up and went to her. She put her hand on her shoulder and spoke in a soft voice. 'Mama, please – please forgive my dad. Remember you taught me to forgive those guys that jilted me, uh? Mama, please – for the Lord's own sake, please –!'

Romoke was deeply moved. A tear slowly rolled down her face. There was a long silence of deep meditation. Francis bowed his head; likewise did Funso.

'Francis,' Romoke spoke at last – 'hmm, because God also forgives us when we do wrong, I… I forgive you… I forgive you – I forgive you, Francis!' And she burst into tears. She went to him and took him up.

'Thank you, Romoke. Thank you for forgiving me,' Francis said as he wiped tears from his own eyes too.

Oh, the solemnity of the reunion! Oh, the tranquility of the reconciliation!

After a moment of thoughtful tears, they all sat up to discuss, but now, on more intimate terms.

'You see, Romoke, we both got our deserved punishment for our bad pasts –even Felicia my wife, whom you said have lured you into being morally corrupt in your secondary school days. We all didn't escape nemesis,' remarked Francis. 'I suffered the loss of my dear wife and was also partly paralysed with stroke as my nemesis. Felicia lost her life as the consequence for her wrongs. You lost your womb as yours,' he explained.

'But what gives me satisfaction', Romoke put in, 'is not at all that Felicia met her nemesis and died – no; but that she had turned to God before she died!'

'Yes, that's it!' exclaimed Francis. 'Our joy is that we are new people with new lives – with a new testimony!'

* * *

After about thirty minutes of talking, the air was now devoid of heaviness.

'I think nothing's stopping us from beginning to make plans for their marriage. Let's just talk a little about the dates for the Introduction ceremony,the Engagement ceremony and the wedding,' Romoke suggested.

'Now?' queried Francis. 'But… but – well, if you say so,' he said. 'All right, maybe I should ask Funso and Yemisi – When do you two plan to get wedded? I mean, when do you wish it should be?'

Funso adjusted his sitting posture and the gleam in his eyes showed enthusiasm. 'To say my mind sir, I'll like it to be around May, this year,' he said.

'*Haba*[100] Funso, you're too much in a hurry! We're just in March!' said Yemisi.

---

100 Come on.

'Now Yemisi,' Funso said, 'we've been courting since February – won't four months courtship be OK?' he queried.

'OK, when do you prefer then, Yemisi?' enquired Francis.

'To be candid, I'd prefer it to be next year,' said Yemisi.

'*HABA*!!!' exclaimed Funso. 'Two thousand and nine! What'll you be waiting for!?'

'That's a medical mind for you!' Francis joked. 'They've got little time to think on these things we spend our lives on! They spend their time studying their gigantic medical textbooks!'

They pealed with laughter. Then Francis turned to Yemisi. 'Look Yemisi, candidly, that date is too far, at least you should consider that you both aren't getting any younger.'

'What about having it in December?' Yemisi suggested.

'It's still too far!' said Funso.

'Ha! Funso! You want us to get wedded *today*?' Yemisi joked. 'You're too much in a hurry as if it should just be now!'

'Don't mind us men – everything about us is always immediate especially when it comes to marrying a woman,' remarked Francis jokingly. 'Don't mind Funso, he doesn't want to agree with the elders that the bridegroom to whom his bride is being brought to stay doesn't need to be in anxious longings!' he added.

'But Dad, I think I see his point,' said Yemisi. 'Actually, if I were Funso – a thirty-one year old, going to be thirty-two; already engaged for two months now – I think if I were him I'd even be more in a hurry to get wedded than he is!'

They laughed.

'So why are you now keeping me waiting, Sweetheart, when you know you'd even do more than me if you were in my shoes?' Funso teased.

'Don't worry, I now agree that we should have the wedding sooner, I suggest August,' replied Yemisi.

'Wow!' Funso burst out. Then his voice dropped. 'Comes from your heart?'

'From my heart!'

'You sure?'

'Course, I'm sure!'

'GREAT!!!' Funso burst out and wriggled around in a thrill of excitement.

They chortled with delight except Romoke, who was sitting quiet.

Funso stopped short and turned to her. 'Mum, what's wrong again? You ain't saying nothing.'

Romoke let out a deep sigh and then spoke.

'Mr. Olorunsanmi and Yemisi, I know I've contributed to whatever misfortune your family might have experienced. It is now I remember how I might have done so. Let me narrate it. After my operation in May 1981 and I was discharged from the hospital only to discover Francis had fled, I resolved to commit suicide. While I was in the bush where I wanted to poison myself, I made some serious pronouncements; I issued some terrible curses against Francis. I said I cursed Francis; I said my womb cursed him; I said the foetus he got me to abort cursed him. But I never could fathom the weight of those words and the extent to which they'd work to bring misfortunes against not only Francis, but Francis' nuclear family!

'Now I understand better the deeper meaning of the words of that curse, Francis. That my soul cursed you, meant I cursed your person; that my womb cursed you, meant I cursed the maternity of your wife; and that the foetus you got me to abort cursed you, meant I cursed the child that would be born by your wife!'

She stood up and raised a hand to the heavens.

'Now that I have forgiven you – I stand on the Word of God that whatever I loose on earth shall be loosed in Heaven, and I cancel this curse now and destroy its power and hold on you Francis Olorunsanmi and your family in the mighty name of Jesus Christ!'

'Amen!!!' they all responded.

It was as if Yemisi's eyes had been unveiled over something.

'Ha! I see why I had had recurring broken relationships!' she said.

'My dear,' said Romoke, 'I never intended to cause you Yemisi the misfortune. If I'd known that you would be Francis' child, I wouldn't have placed the curse, perhaps. But we thank God He has bought reconciliation between your dad and me, and that the curse is now cancelled by faith; and you can be sure it can never have effect on you or on your dad anymore!'

'I want to believe so,' said Yemisi.

'No don't be trying to believe so; you can rest assured I can never cease to love you – you're the love of my life!' Funso said with enthusiasm.

Yemisi chuckled.

'You believe? You relaxed now?' said Funso.

'Yes, Funso!' smiled Yemisi.

* * *

On one Saturday in August 2008, the street of a grand cathedral in Ikaodọgba town was filled to capacity.

The pipe organ in the cathedral began to play as the congregation stood up to sing a hymn; and then the clergy began to file out. Then, you could see the bride and the groom filing out arm in arm, with the best man, the bridesmaid and the whole bridal train filing along behind them in nuptial elegance.

It was the wedding of Funso and Yemisi and then they walked away from the altar as Mr. and Dr. (Mrs.) Bayetiri – the latest couple at that very time! Funso was dressed in a white shirt and a silvery grey suit, and with a black bow tie with silver polka dots; and he had on a pair of shiny black loafers. Yemisi was dressed in a long, flowing, immaculate white wedding gown. She had on a beautiful pair of earings and a beaded necklace, and her hair remained a mass of curls. Really, she was so seraphic in her flowing white gown.

As the new couples elegantly walked out of the cathedral arm in arm, followed by the bridal train and then the congregation, the band outside began to play on their trumpets and their drums.

Funso looked into Yemisi's attractive eyes for quite a while as they danced to the band's music. He gazed with feelings that were indeed deep and inexpressible. And then he beamed a seraphic smile at her and she smiled back serenely. And as if that wasn't enough, he embraced his beautiful bride and gave her a kiss on the lips; and the crowd gave a loud shout of excitement.

10

Joy Again

From inside a delivery room in the Federal Government Hospital in Iga town emanated the groans of Mrs. Yemisi Bayetiri in labour pains. It was then ten minutes before midnight that Thursday, the twenty-eighth of May, 2009. She had been in labour for about six hours and she was becoming very weak. His husband Funso was pacing outside the delivery room, extremely disturbed and discomposed. Romoke was seated beside him, anxious.

Now at this point of our story, Romoke had now completed her master's correspondence course in Mass Communication and was now working as a lecturer of Mass Communication in The Federal Polytechnic, in that Iga town, since late 2008. However, she was not going to stop on that step of the academic ladder. She was not going to stop with master's degree; she was in fact going to proceed to have a PhD. Now, it is clear and evident that Romoke's point of weakness before was now indeed a point of strength!

Now, the doctor that was in charge of Yemisi's delivery

came out of the delivery room. Funso rushed to him, asking a hundred and one questions. 'How's it, Doctor? Will my wife deliver safely? Is she all right? Is she going to –?'

'Calm down, Mr. Bayetiri,' the doctor cut in. And then he spoke calmly. 'You see, I'm afraid, she might need Caesarean section'

Funso turned with open mouth to Romoke, who at that same time stared at him with her two hands laid on her head. They both understand why Caesarean section was a no-go area for Yemisi. It wasn't merely because of its natural risks, which may not be an alarming thing if the operation is properly carried out; after all, there are a great many successful Caesareans. Moreover, it wasn't that Yemisi had a rare blood group or had some related things, that they were so deeply apprehensive about the Caesarean. But then, it dawned on them both that bad history was about to repeat itself. They remembered that Yemisi's mother, Felicia, had died after being delivered of her by a Caesarean section. The question then was: Were the terrible consequences of all Francis did to Romoke on campus in 1981 – were they not over yet? Would they continue without an end?

Funso turned to the doctor again. 'Does she know? Have you told her that a Caesarean is likely to be the only way out?'

The doctor chuckled.

'She knows that already, being a medical practitioner herself. But anyway, I've let her know quite a while ago that she must have to go through a Caesarean section, and it's just now she consented to my piece of advice that she should have the operation.'

'Ha! She consented! Good God!' exclaimed Funso. He became confused.

'What else do you want her to do?' the doctor chuckled. 'Goodness! She's got no option than to do just that; and mind you, Caesarean section is not as risky as many of you people think. Look, there's no cause for alarm. In any case, she asked me to encourage you that all's going to be well, and that you should consent to the carrying out of the operation.'

Funso stood there staring blankly at the doctor as tears gathered in his eyes. Romoke too stared at Funso, waiting to hear his next words. Funso stared for a while, and then with a shaky voice he said, 'Carry out the Caesarean,' and a tear rolled down his eyes.

The doctor was moved and he patted him on the shoulder. 'Don't worry; it's going to be successful, God willing,' he said.

So, the doctor showed him into the room where he would sign.

Romoke had taken mobile phone and dialled Francis, who was at that time in the town. Francis had come to Iga on a four-day conference that was holding in a luxury hotel where he, together with other delegates, was lodged. The conference was on democracy and which was to mark Nigeria's Democracy Day which has been every 29th May, since 1999. Francis Olorunsanmi was among the delegates of the conference which had been holding since Wednesday, 27th May. They were to round off the conference on Saturday morning with a banquet, in which personalities in Nigerian democracy were going to give talks.

Francis picked up Romoke's call. She told him that Yemisi (who he knew was already in the delivery room) was going to have a Caesarean, and he became apprehensive. But there was nothing he could do to help it, for she had to have it if she wasn't going to lose her life in the course of the prolonged labour. He told Romoke to call him again when Yemisi would have had the operation, to inform him of the outcome; and he really prayed it would be successful. They ended the conversation.

Now, Funso, in the hospital, had finished signing, and the doctors were then getting their surgical apparatus ready. And then, lo and behold, everybody heard her at once groaned loudly with all her strength. And then after, they could no more hear her groan! She had ceased! Oh, she had ceased to groan! But then, the cry of a new-born baby pervaded the entire place! A baby was born! It was ten past twelve.

Funso was excited and felt as if his body had suddenly become light, so much that he jumped here and there like a little boy. He felt like breaking the door of the delivery room open and dashing inside; for he was overjoyed!

Then while they were still jubilating, at about fifteen minutes past twelve, Yemisi made another deep but loud groan; and this time around, with all the strength left in her; and, lo and behold, another cry of a baby joined the first, and the whole place was pervaded with deafening cries of twin babies!

What inexpressible joy filled their heart! Absolutely overjoyed Funso was! Now he had become a daddy of twins, and Yemisi his wife, the Mother of Twins! Beautiful! Really it is!

* * *

Now it was 4 o'clock in the morning and Romoke had not called Francis to tell him anything. Actually, she had been dialling him all the while, but there was network failure, so she couldn't just get through calling him. Francis had also been trying to call her to enquire about the operation.

And as early as six in the morning, Francis got into his car and set out heading for the Federal Government Hospital. He sped all the way. Now when nearing the hospital, he stopped at an ATM centre and withdrew a sum of fifty thousand naira, to help with the necessary hospital charges, especially that of the Caesarean section – for he thought Yemisi would have had it. He got back into his car and drove on.

When he got to the hospital, with the help of a certain nurse, he was able to locate Yemisi's ward. He held onto the door handle of the ward for a while, took a few breaths to calm him and then opened the door.

The first thing that greeted him was Yemisi's seraphic smile. She was lying on the hospital bed. Beside her at her head was Funso sitting and fondling her ear. On the other side of the bed was seated Romoke on a chair. And then beside Yemisi at Funso's side, were two cradles, each with each of the twin babies, sleeping peacefully. A baby boy and a baby girl!

'Ah! Thank God!' Francis breathed.

'Congrats, Mr. Olorunsanmi!' said Romoke. 'You're now a grandpa – a grandpa of twins! A baby boy and a baby girl!'

He was absolutely delighted. He rushed to the cradles and gazed at the twin babies, and then he looked at Funso and Yemisi. 'Thank God!' he beamed.

Yemisi sat up, resting her back against the pillow. 'Dad,' she said, 'I delivered naturally and not by Caesarean!'

'Eh! Goodness me!' Francis burst out.

'Have your seat, Daddy,' said Funso, offering him a seat, and he sat.

'Funso!' Francis said.

'Yes sir?' he replied.

'Baba Ibeji![101] Congrats!'

'Thank you sir!'

'You and your wife have played a one-all draw!' joked Francis.

'Daddy, I don't get,' chuckled Funso.

'You've got a boy and a girl –you both scored same points, didn't you?'

They laughed.

---

101 Daddy of twins!

'Let me inform mama at home that Yemisi had given birth safely,' Romoke said as she dialled Segilola mobile number; for the network was back to normal.

'That's right; inform grandma,' said Funso.

Segilola's phone rang but the call wasn't picked up. She dialled the number again and it rang, but again it wasn't picked up.

'Mama didn't pick it up,' said Romoke – 'I'm sure she left it inside her bag. That's what mama does – whether she's at home or she's out, she'll always zip up her phone inside her handbag; and many times when she's at home she'll lock the bag inside the wardrobe! Tell me how she will hear!'

Funso chuckled. 'Don't blame her; maybe she's not got used to using a mobile yet – remember it was this year you got it for her.'

'I got it for her January; normally, she ought to have got used to it by now – this is May!' said Romoke.

'Never mind, mama; try her again,' said Yemisi.

Romoke dialled her number again.

Now, Segilola had put her mobile phone on the table in the living room and she was in her bedroom. Actually, she had been hearing her mobile ring in the sitting room, with a musical ringing tone; but she had thought that the music was from the radio, which had been on but had ceased working because of the power failure. She then thought, each time she heard the ringing, that the electric power was then back, and so the radio which was already on started to work! Now, this time around, she decided to go and turn off the supposed radio lest the unstable electricity damaged it!

She got to the living room while her mobile was still ringing. She rushed to it and picked it up. 'Hallo,' she said.

'Mama, where did you leave your phone?' queried Romoke, rather loudly.

'Don't mind me; I left it here in the living room,' replied Segilola. 'Is this Romoke?'

'Yes ma.'

'Ha Romoke! How's Yemisi?'

'Mama, it is good news!'

'Tell me; tell me the good news!'

'Mama, Yemisi has given birth safely!'

'Ha! *A dupẹ!* [102]'

'Mama, *ọmọ meji lantilanti!* [103]'

'*Ibeji? Kaṣa!*'[104]

'Yes, mama!'

'Ha! Are you with her there?'

'Yes, ma; we're all here with her in the hospital.'

'OK, give the phone to her; let me congratulate her.'

'All right.'

She gave it to Yemisi and she took over.

'Hello, mama.'

'Ha, Oluwayemisi! *O ku ewu ọmọ!* '[105]

'Thank you, mama. I should congratulate you too that you're living to see your great grandchildren! Congrats, mama.'

'Thank you, my daughter. You're right; our people say that children are the crown of the elders. I'm really happy to be alive to see my great grandchildren coming into the world. Perhaps it is so as to see this joy that God has preserved my life till now despite the hardships I've faced. Now, when will the doctors discharge you?'

---

102 We thank God.
103 Two bouncing babies.
104 Twins? Wow.
105 Congratulations on your delivery.

'By Sunday evening I should be discharged.'

'Oh, I just can't wait to see the twins! Now, let me say some prayers for you, my daughter.'

'OK, mama.'

'Oluwayemisi, you will be fruitful and blessed in the house of your husband. You will be called favoured in the courtyard of your in-laws. Your children and your children's children will call you blessed. And you will be your husband's delight till the end of your lives!'

'Amen! Amen! Thank you, mama.'

'My dear, let me stop for now; when you return I will bless you more and also carry the twins in my arms and bless them. I'm eager to see them!'

'Thank you, mama.'

'Bye-bye.'

'Bye, mama!' She gave the phone back to Romoke and then took a deep breath. 'Dad, today's my birthday!' she said, smiling.

'Ha! That's true!' exclaimed Francis. 'I've totally forgotten!'

'I know you have!'

'Don't mind me – you know, old age!' Francis joked. 'Happy birthday – on your delivery! Ha-ha!'

They cheered and said happy birthday to her; and then there was a brief silence. Francis spoke, after taking a deep breath.

'Mm, it is twenty-seven years today that I lost my dear wife Felicia.'

'Mmm!' everyone breathed and there was a moment's silence.

'But then today,' continued Francis, 'God compensates me with this beautiful birth!' he beamed.

'Really, May the twenty-ninth is really a significant date to us,' said Romoke. 'I can remember that Friday, 29th May, 1981 – my world came crashing down in front of me! But then, I can't forget that prophetic word to me that is now fulfilled today: "Not only will you be a mother again, but also, a grandmother." Then, I couldn't grasp how that could be possible; but today, it's come true!'

She paused a bit.

'Mm, who could imagine that Mr. Olorunsanmi and me could be reconciled this way? Who could tell that the daughter of my most-hated enemy then would now become my daughter-in-law? Ha-ha! This is great! You couldn't have fathomed it!'

'Really!' said Francis.

She turned to him.

'Francis, see the good Divine Providence has to bring out of all that had happened! We both never knew when you left campus in 1981 that Providence would make our paths cross again, through our children! Ah, now I understand what my mother told me in 1993, which sounded like a riddle then. She told me: "Take good care of Funso. He's going to make your dreams come true and also bring sweetness out of the fountain that had brought you bitterness. Through him, the cat and the mouse will no longer have a predatory relationship, for the first time in their interaction." That's exactly what she said. Mm, I now see!'

Funso put his hand in Yemisi's hand and said, 'Mum, really it's amazing how our young love brought an end to the long-standing hatred between you and Daddy Olorunsanmi. We just looked on and watched love conquer hurt and resentment! Remember I told you many waters can't quench love! It's stronger than death; let alone hatred, I guess!'

'But mama, you know something?' Yemisi put in.'When I was jilted the second time and I met you that Christmas,and told you my misery – you know what gave my life a new blossoming so quickly? It was the hope I got from your story you told me then. And now, I can even see for myself from your life, that there's hope for a person even when they've been "felled" and are completely "reduced to a stump"; cos they can still sprout again! So wonderful!'

'Yes, my dear,' Romoke smiled; 'really wonderful!'